Illustrators

15

Editor:
Gerald McConnell

Designer:
Howard Munce

Hastings House Publishers
New York

The Fifteenth Annual National
Exhibition of Illustration held in
the Galleries of the Society of
Illustrators, 128 East 63rd Street,
New York, N.Y., February 14
through April 6, 1972.

Contents

COMMITTEE 15

Chairman	James Crowell
Ass't Chairman	Robert Cuevas
Call for Entries Designer	James Crowell
Announcement Designer	Victor Valla
Hanging Chairman	James Consor
Luncheon Chairman	Robert Cuevas
Luncheon Speakers	Arnold Copeland Dr. Bill Martin Jerome Snyder
Treasurer	Charles McVicker
Exhibition Staff	Fern Ramos Cathy Groff Norma Pimsler Shirley Crowell Arpi Ermoyan

ISBN: 8038-3393-8

Library of Congress Catalog Card Number: 59-10849

Printed in the United States of America

Distributors:
CANADA   Saunders of Toronto, Ltd., Don Mills, Ontario
GREAT BRITAIN AND THE COMMONWEALTH   Constable & Co., Ltd., 10 Orange Street, London WC 2
AUSTRIA, GERMANY AND SWITZERLAND   Aurthur Niggli, Ltd., Böhl, 9052 Niederteufen AR, Switzerland
FRANCE   Editions Parallèles, 172 rue Pelleport, Paris XXe
All other countries   Fleetbooks c/o Feffer and Simons, Inc., 31 Union Square, New York 10003

Anniversaries are
symbolized by materials:
Gold, Silver, etc.
Crystal is the stuff for Fifteen.

Illustrators 15

The President's Message

As we plunge forward on our individual careers, whether it be trying to make one big splash, struggling to stay afloat or diving for medals, this publication affords us an annual opportunity to thrust our heads above water and to see whither we are bound collectively. As an aid to sharpen our vision, great care is focused upon screening the submissions to secure the finest representatives of the many currents of aesthetic trends on the contemporary scene, without artificial trendsetting. We have endeavored to make the images in this volume speak for themselves as to where we are in the history of illustration. Therefore with minimal editorializing it is for you the reader to digest, interpret and absorb what is relevant and meaningful to you. The most valid conclusions may be your own. There are visions to delight and ponder in the succeeding pages. I hope you will enjoy our newborn 15th offspring.

For the Society and for myself I would like to express our gratitude to, and pride in, the chairman, his committee, the designer and editor, the staff and all those who submitted entries to this exhibition.

Shannon Stirnweis

Herb Tauss

The Editor □ Gerald McConnell

Paul Calle

This is the Fifteenth edition of the Society of Illustrators Annual. To call it a milestone is an oversimplification, for when one stops to realize that all the people who worked so hard on each of the fifteen shows and editions did so willingly, giving of their time and effort out of love for the profession, — it is more like a miracle. We have been fortunate all these years to have such a far-sighted membership.

A list of editors and designers of the past annuals is a very impressive one. These are the men who have contributed so heavily to its continued success.

Each year the designer takes on the total responsibility for designing a 300 page annual including an average of 500 illustrations — this, within a minimal time allotment and an even smaller budget, while his own work is building up in the corner of his studio.

The one single person who has followed all 15 annuals through this process has been our publisher, Russell Neale. He has been our guiding light, along with his staff at Hastings House. They have been patient, informative and gentle, but above all else they have been dedicated to the cause of illustration and to this Annual. For this the Society gives Russell Neale, his staff and all the contributing Society members a deep and heartfelt thanks, as I'm sure artists all over the world who own even just *one* of these Annuals.

The Chairman

Jerry Pinkney

James Crowell

The Designer □ Howard Munce

Bernie Fuchs

The Illustrator's most creative time, in most cases, is during his first years as art student and Illustrator. He is constantly dealing with unknowns and forced into new personal discoveries. He is in a creative state of mind, resulting in a product original from the one that preceded it. He is able to see the familiar as unique.

In time, through repetition, he develops his mechanical skills and acquires experience. He becomes capable of producing a high percentage of successfully completed works—he is now a professional.

Creativity and professionalism; at first consideration they seem to be completely opposed to each other. One deals with a high degree of certainty, while the other with uncertainty (the intuitive).

Here then is a basic challenge to the Illustrator. Everytime he begins a new assignment, to somehow blend and profit from both—to guard against relying totally on skills already mastered or experiences already experienced—and to retain rather then repress his intuitive responses.

The Annual Exhibition of Illustration is an acknowledgement of those Illustrators who have been able to resolve that challenge.

Laying out this fat tome would be far easier if one dwelt in a dirigible hangar.

I began by placing 531 8x10 glossies on the floor. In my house that takes up the studio, a guest room, the so-called playroom, a john and a flight of stairs. It also takes up a lot of time.

It also caused my cat to flee. And his fleas to flee with him.

I strolled endlessly, head down, among the prints searching for an overall premise upon which to base the groupings and page arrangements.

Unconsciously, I hummed *Tiptoe Through The Tulips* on my winding journey.

I will spare the world the remaining details, first because nobody cares and secondly because it will be somebody's job to find a designer for *next* year's Annual.

The type is **Aster,** a relatively new face —which is more than I can say for my own.

The Judges & Juries:

Editorial

John Moodie, Chairman
Richard Anderson
Paul Giovanopoulos
Ted Coconis
John Groth
Richard Harvey
Mitchell Hooks
Walter Einsel
Susan Obrant

Book

Victor Valla, Chairman
Edwin Broussard
Joan Fenton
Walter Hortens
Doug Johnson
Bob Jones
Mike Mitchell
Charles Santore

Honoré Daumier

Advertising

Robert Geissmann, Chairman
Betty Fraser
Seymour Chwast
William Hofmann
Arnold Holeywell
Robert Lavin
Martin Pedersen
Paul Williams

Institutional

Murray Tinkelman, Chairman
Richard Amsel
Robert Cunningham
Robert Hallock
Blake Hampton
Tom Lovell
Michael Naki
Jerry Pinkney
J. C. Suares

This perky bronze monarch stands in the center of a circular table in the Society's dining room. The table is designated as King Arthur's Round Table.

The King is Brownie. Brownie was Arthur William Brown, an illustrious illustrator of the past. He was President then Honorary President almost forever.

The Society was his second home—and everyone who encountered him there was warmed and made welcome by this cordial, nice man.

Sculpture by Irma Selz

128 East 63rd Street, New York City, U.S.A.

This Society is 73 years old. It has been in this building since 1938. Though it is a place of varied activities, they all have but one ultimate purpose: to celebrate and advance the art of illustration.

Past Presidents of the Society of Illustrators

1901 **W.T. Smedley**
by Norman Price

1902 **A.B. Wenzell**
by Adolph Treidler

1903 **Arthur I. Keller**
by George Brehm

1904-1905 **Charles Dana Gibson**
by William Oberhardt

1926-27 **George Wright**
by Frank Bensing

1927-29 **C.D. Williams**
by James Montgomery Flagg

1929-36 **Wallace Morgan**
by William Oberhardt

1936-38 **Denys Wortman**
by William Oberhardt

1948-51 **Harvey Dunn**
by Steven Kidd

1951-53 **William H. Schneider**
by William Oberhardt

1953-55 Robert Geissmann
by William Oberhardt

1955-56 **Howard Munce**
by Austin Briggs

1960-61 **Tran Mawicke**
by John Gannam

1961-63 **Steven Dohanos**
by C.C. Beall

1963-64 **John Moodie**
by Bernie Fuchs

1964-65 **Carl Bobertz**
by Al Schmidt

1906 **Daniel Carter Beard**
by S. J. Woolf

1907-1908 **Albert E. Sterner**
by William Oberhardt

1921 **Edward Penfield**
by C. D. Williams

1922-26 **Dean Cornwell**
by Charles Dana Gibson

1938-41 **Harold Von Schmidt**
by James Montgomery Flagg

1941-44 **John Holmgren**
by Martha Sawyers

1944-47 **Arthur Wm. Brown**
by Al Parker

1947-48 **Albert Dorne**
by William Oberhardt

1956-57 **Ervine Metzl**
by Ray Prohaska

1957-58 **Charles Henry Carter**
by William Oberhardt

1958-59 **Ray Prohaska**
by John Groth

1959-60 **George Shealy**
by Woodi Ishmael

1965-67 **Barye W. Phillips**
by Paul Calle

1967-68 **David K. Stone**
by Coby Whitmore

1968-70 **Wesley B. McKeown**
by Norman Rockwell

1970-72 **Walter Brooks**
by Clark Hulings

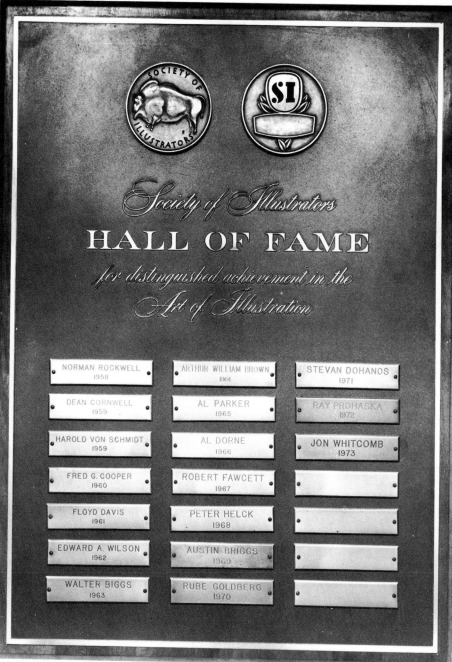

Society of Illustrators

HALL OF FAME

for distinguished achievement in the
Art of Illustration

NORMAN ROCKWELL 1958	ARTHUR WILLIAM BROWN 1964	STEVAN DOHANOS 1971
DEAN CORNWELL 1959	AL PARKER 1965	RAY PROHASKA 1972
HAROLD VON SCHMIDT 1959	AL DORNE 1966	JON WHITCOMB 1973
FRED G. COOPER 1960	ROBERT FAWCETT 1967	
FLOYD DAVIS 1961	PETER HELCK 1968	
EDWARD A. WILSON 1962	AUSTIN BRIGGS 1969	
WALTER BIGGS 1963	RUBE GOLDBERG 1970	

David Blossom, winner of the 1973 Hamilton King Award. See p. 29

The Hamilton King Award

Each year since the early sixties the Society has been giving an award to one of its own members for the best illustration in this show. It is fitting that it be given under the name of Hamilton King.

King was born in Lewiston, Maine, in 1871. His family later moved to Newark, N.J. At thirteen, he dropped out of school. He then got a job in an architect's office because, as he said afterwards, there he could steal all the pencils and paper he needed for his drawing.

In his late teens Hamilton worked for the New York Sun as an artist-reporter. He soon sold drawings to Truth Magazine and then rapidly progressed to become a leader among the magazine artists of the day. He also created many brilliant theatrical posters during the early 1900's.

Some previous winners of the Hamilton King Award include **Paul Calle, Bernie Fuchs, Robert Peak, Mark English, Alan Cober, Ray Ameijide.**

The Hall of Fame

In every line of endeavor, there are standouts. Whether they be a Maria Callas or Willie Mays, the very execution of their chosen profession may be described as a star performance. It is to honor these people that the concept of the Hall of Fame was established.

The Society of Illustrators' Hall of Fame began in 1958. The nominating committee is made up of former Presidents of the Society. The 1973 selection of Jon Whitcomb recognizes one of the most successful careers in American illustration. For years his sparkling illustrations lit up the pages of magazines across the nation. More recently he has divided his time between portraiture and outsized acrylic constructions. Jon joins an august list: **Norman Rockwell, Dean Cornwell, Harold Von Schmidt, Fred C Cooper, Floyd Davis, Edward A. Wilson, Walter Biggs, Arthur William Brown, Al Parker, Al Dorne, Robert Fawcett, Peter Helck, Austin Briggs, Rube Goldberg, Steve Dohanos and Ray Prohaska.**

Willis Pyle *Chairman*

1 Advertising
Artist/**Norman Rockwell**
Art Director/Acy Lehman
Client/RCA Records

2 Book
Artist/**Hector Garrido**
Art Director/Barbara Bertoli
Title/Holding Wonder
Publisher/Avon Books

4 Institutional
Artist/**Karen Noles**
Art Director/Norma Haynes
Agency/Buzza
Client/Buzza

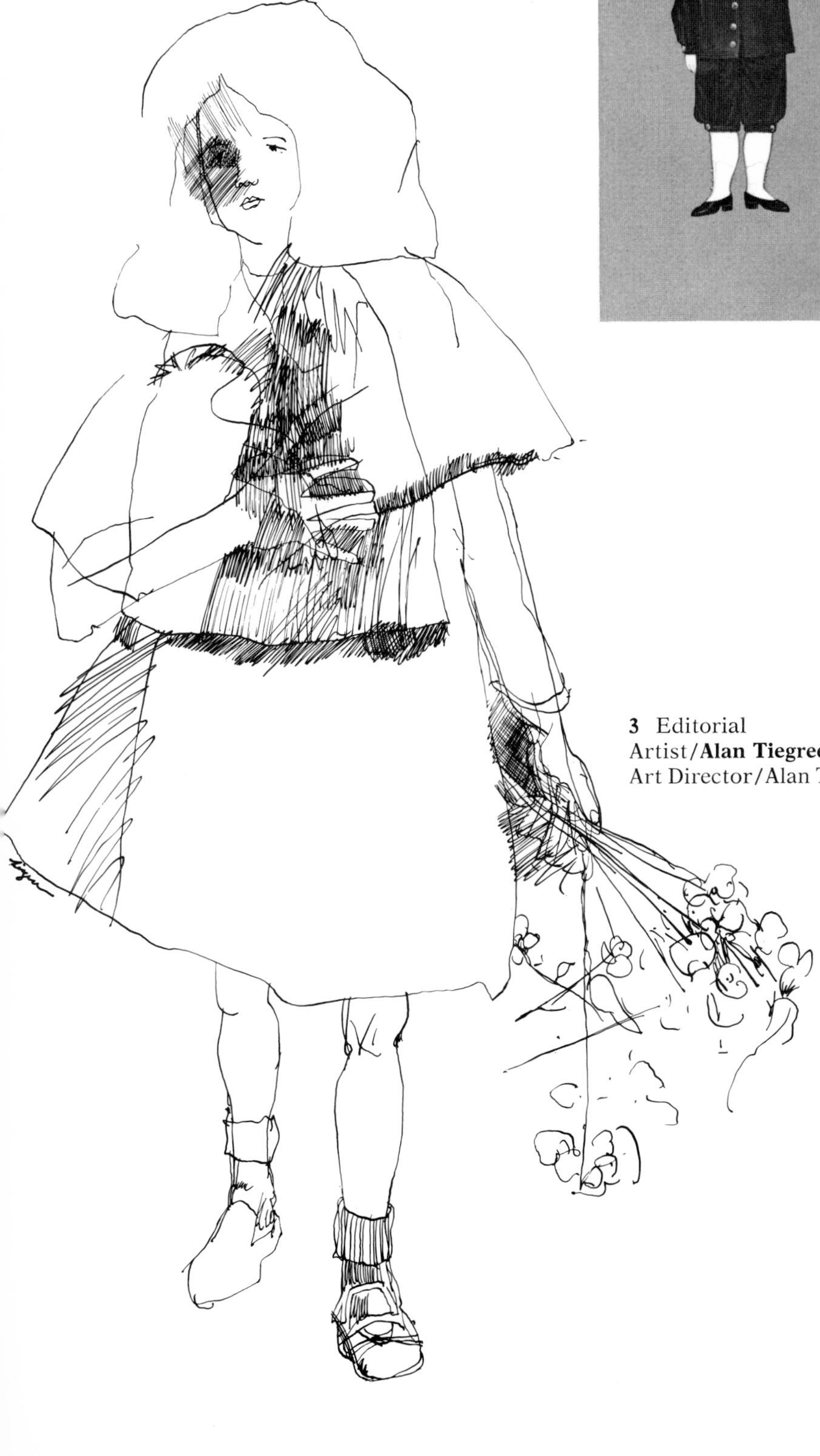

3 Editorial
Artist/**Alan Tiegreen**
Art Director/Alan Tiegreen

5 Institutional
Artist/**Sharleen Pederson**
Art Director/Ron Wolin
Agency/Ron Wolin Co.
Client/Art Directors Club of Los Angeles
■ **Award of Excellence**

Volume I
THE
NIGHT LAND
$1.25

"In all the literature of fantasy, there are few works so
sheerly, purely creative as THE NIGHT LAND."—Clark Ashton Smith

William Hope Hodgson
Introduction   by Lin Carter

"...HE NIGHT LAND is a tale of the remote future—billions
...years after the death of the sun. It is one of the most
...otent pieces of macabre imagination ever written...there
...a sense of cosmic alienage, breathless mystery, and terri-
...ed expectancy unrivalled in the whole range of literature."
—H. P. Lovecraft

THE NIGHT LAND
William Hope Hodgson

Volume I

Ballantine Books 02669·1·125

345·02669·1·125

Cover printed in USA

6 Book
Artist/**Robert LoGrippo**
Art Director/Bob Blanchard
Title/Night Land, Volume 1
Publisher/Ballantine Books, Inc.
■ **Gold Medal**

7 Advertising
Artist/**Joe Isom**
Art Director/Mike Oberlander
Client/West Agro Chemical, Inc.

8 Advertising
Artist/**George S. Gaadt**
Art Director/Ron Chory
Agency/Ketchum, MacLeod & Grove, Inc.
Client/Alcoa

9 Editorial
Artist/**Paul Hogarth**
Art Director/Arthur Paul & Bob Post
Publication/Playboy Magazine

10 Advertising
Artist/**Gerry Gersten**
Art Director/Bob Steigleman
Agency/Young & Rubicam, Inc.
Client/New York Telephone

11 Book
Artist/**Ronald Lehew**
Art Director/Dhyana Hollingsworth
Title/How Does It Feel to Live Next To a Giraffe
Publisher/Holt, Rinehart & Winston, Inc.

How does it feel to live next door to a giraffe?

BY KATHY MANDRY
AND JOE TOTO

illustrated by Ronald LeHew

12 Book
Artist/**Charles Mikolaycak**
Art Director/Robert G. Lowe
Title/The Gorgon's Head
Publisher/Little, Brown and Co.

13 Book
Artist/**Robert Andrew Parker**
Art Director/Edward Aho
Title/Liam's Catch
Publisher/The Viking Press

14 Advertising
Artist/**Chuck Wilkenson**
Art Director/Arlan Ettinger

15 Advertising
Artist/**Gerry Gersten**
Art Director/Diana Graham & Henry Epstein
Client/ABC Television

A. GROSS VEGETATIVE MORPHOLOGY

Juvenile Leaves

Mature Leaves

Petiole

Condensed Root

Condensed Stem

B. LONGITUDINAL SECTION

Cut Petioles

Condensed Stem

Epidermis

Pith

Region of Xylem and Phloem

Cortex

Rootlets

Epidermis   Cortex

Secondary Vascular Tissue

Pith Tissue

C. TRANSVERSE SECTION

RAPHANUS SATIVUS L.
Garden Radish

17 Editorial
Artist/**David Blossom**
Art Director/Howard Munce
Publication/Medical Times

Thyrotoxicosis Associated with Grave's Disease

Radioisotopic Diagnosis of Pulmonary Disease

If You Were Sick, What Hospital Would You Choose?

Pulmonary Function Tests in Community Hospitals

19 Advertising
Artist/**David Edward Byrd**
Art Director/David Edward Byrd
Client/Triton Gallery

18 Book
Artist/**Frank Bozzo**
Art Director/James K. Davis
Title/A Darkness of Giants
Publisher/Doubleday & Co., Inc.

20 Advertising
Artist/**Edward Sorel**
Art Director/Andrew Kner
Client/The New York Times
■ **Award of Excellence**

21 Book
Artist/**Darrell Wiskur**
Art Director/Jeanne Gleason
Title/Who Takes Baths
Publisher/Scott, Foresman & Co.

22 Book
Artist/**Robert Tallon**
Art Director/Robert Tallon
Title/Zoophabets
Publisher/The Bobbs-Merrill Co., Inc.

23 Editorial
Artist/**Don Weller**
Art Director/Joe Iwanaga
Publication/Human Behavior Magazine

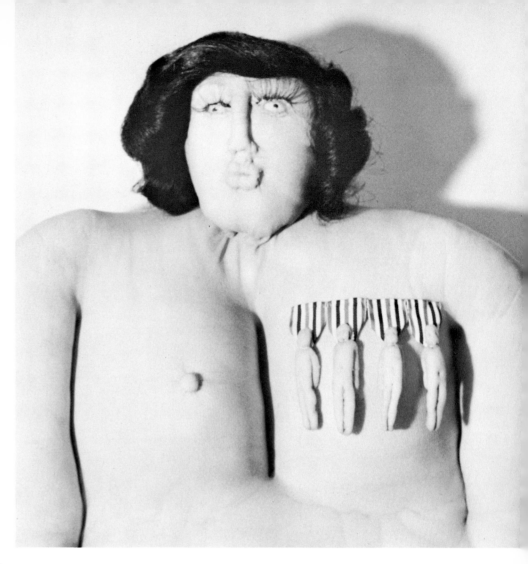

24 Institutional
Artist/**Judith Jampel**
Art Director/Judith Jampel

26 Editorial
Artist/**Dennis Lyall**
Art Director/Dennis Lyall

25 Editorial
Artist/**Eugene Karlin**
Art Director/Doris Crandall
Publication/Cosmopolitan Magazine

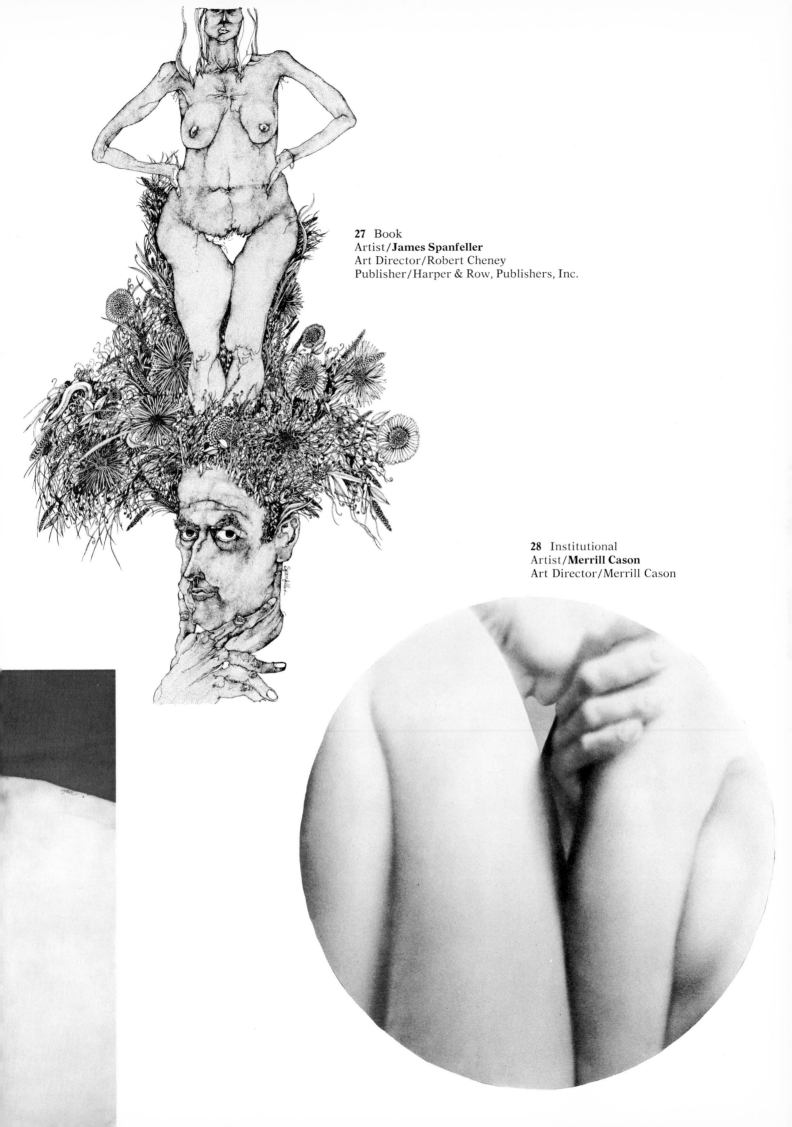

27 Book
Artist/**James Spanfeller**
Art Director/Robert Cheney
Publisher/Harper & Row, Publishers, Inc.

28 Institutional
Artist/**Merrill Cason**
Art Director/Merrill Cason

29 Advertising
Artist/**Alvin J. Pimsler**
Art Director/Dwight Ziegelash
Client/Hubbard Co.

MILWAUKEE COUNTY ZOO FOR CHILDREN

30 Institutional
Artist/**Lois Ehlert**
Art Director/Lois Ehlert
Agency/E. F. Schmidt Co.
Client/Milwaukee County Zoo

31 Editorial
Artist/**Brad Holland**
Art Director/Arthur Paul & Bob Post
Publication/Playboy Magazine

33 Editorial
Artist/**Franz Altschuler**
Art Director/Arthur Paul & Gordon Mortensen
Publication/Playboy

32 Book
Artist/**Ronald Himler**
Art Director/Dorothy M. Hagen
Title/Baby
Publisher/Harper & Row, Publishers, Inc.

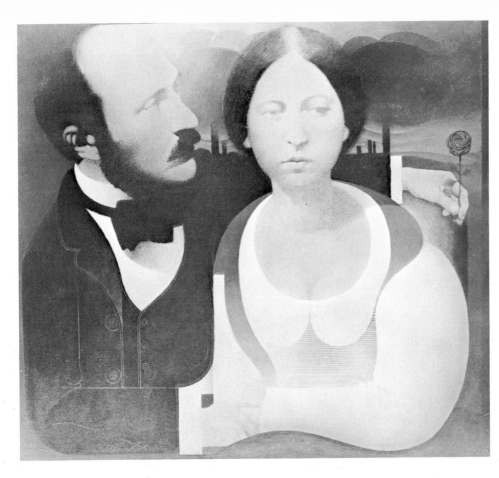

34 Advertising
Artist/**Mark English**
Art Director/Dick Umnitz
Client/Literary Guild
■ **Award of Excellence**

35 Editorial
Artist/**Arthur Lidov**
Art Director/Bernard Springsteel
Publication/Good Housekeeping Magazine

36 Advertising
Artist/**Carol Anthony**
Art Director/Jim Witham & Ralph Moxcey
Agency/Humphrey, Browning & MacDougall
Client/S. D. Warren Paper Co., Inc.

37 Editorial
Artist/**James Barkley**
Art Director/B. Martin Pedersen
Agency/Pedersen Design, Inc.
Publication/American Way Magazine

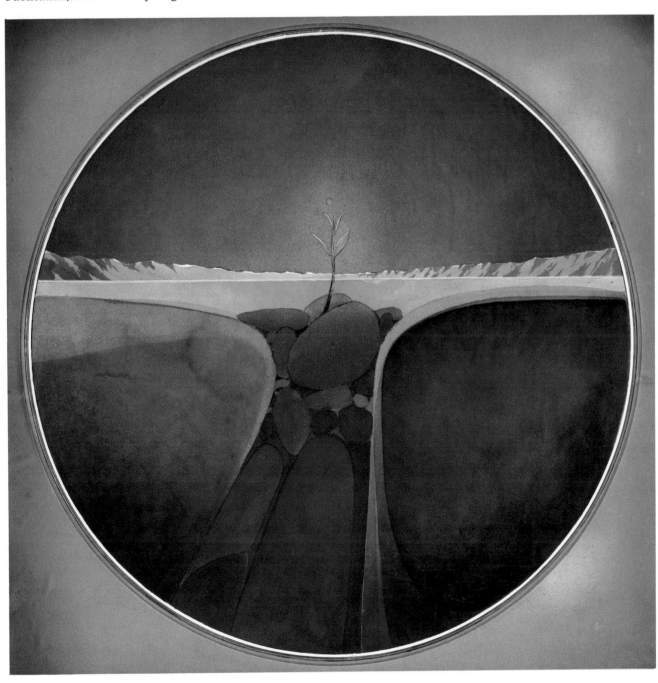

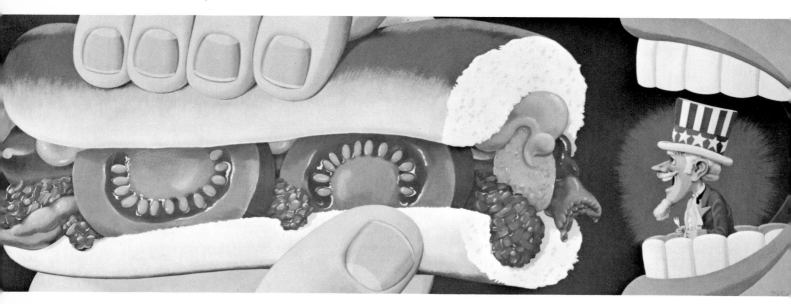

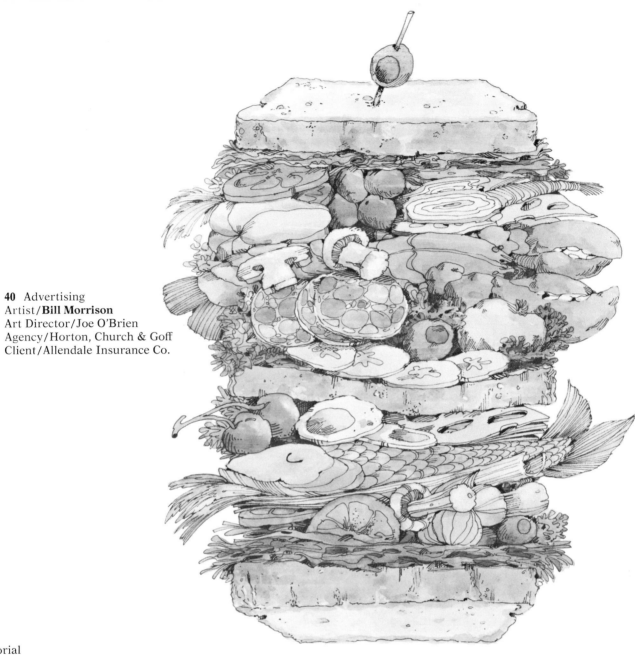

40 Advertising
Artist/**Bill Morrison**
Art Director/Joe O'Brien
Agency/Horton, Church & Goff
Client/Allendale Insurance Co.

41 Editorial
Artist/**Walter Einsel**
Art Director/Harry Redler
Publication/Connecticut Magazine

43 Book
Artist/**Arthur Shilstone**
Art Director/Ken Hine
Title/The Odessa File
Publisher/Reader's Digest Association

42 Book
Artist/**John Overmyer**
Art Director/Harald Peter
Title/I Am My Brother
Publisher/Hallmark Cards, Inc.

44 Editorial
Artist/**Gervasio Gallardo**
Art Director/Gervasio Gallardo

45 Editorial
Artist/**Roger Hane**
Art Director/Alvin Grossman & Modesto Torre
Publication/McCall's Magazine

46 Institutional
Artist/**Doug Gervasi**
Art Director/Doug Gervasi
■ **Award of Excellence**

47 Advertising
Artist/**Marie Michal**
Art Director/Roger Core
Agency/Benton & Bowles Inc.
Client/Proctor & Gamble Distributing Co.

48 Editorial
Artist/**Marcus Hamilton**
Art Director/Marcus Hamilton

49 Institutional
Artist/**Daniel Maffia**
Art Director/Alan J. Klawans
Client/Smith, Kline & French Laboratories

50 Editorial
Artist/**Ed Renfro**
Art Director/Stan R. Corfman
Publication/Marathon World

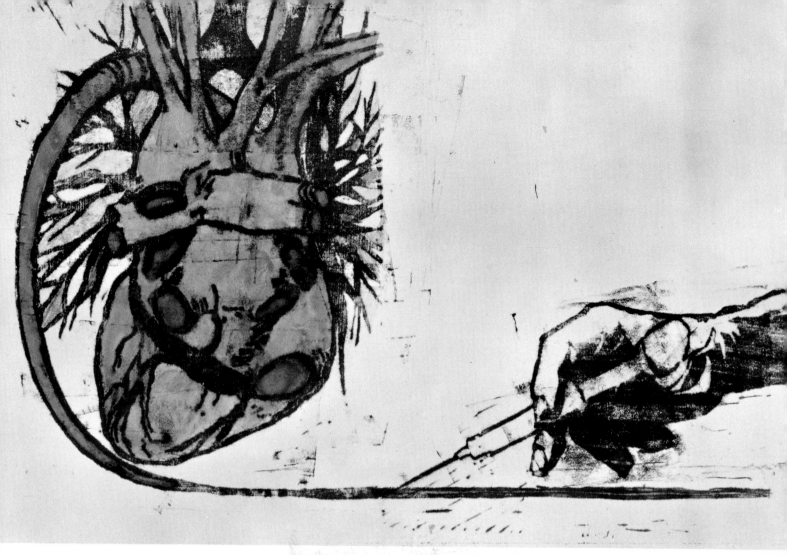

51 Editorial
Artist/**David Passalacqua**
Art Director/Ira Silberlicht
Publication/Emergency Medicine

52 Editorial
Artist/**Doug Johnson**
Art Director/Arthur Paul & Roy Moody
Publication/Playboy Magazine

53 Advertising
Artist/**Don Ivan Punchatz**
Art Director/Art Christy & Frank Perry
Agency/Fuller & Smith & Ross, Inc.
Client/Mobil Oil Co.

55 Institutional
Artist/**David M. Gaadt**
Art Director/David M. Gaadt
Agency/Creative Services, Inc.
Client/Creative Services, Inc.

56 Advertising
Artist/**Gordon Kibbee**
Art Director/Robert L. Heimall
Client/Elektra Records

57 Editorial
Artist/**Albert Williams**
Art Director/Albert Williams

59 Book
Artist/**Joseph A. Smith**
Art Director/Joseph A. Smith

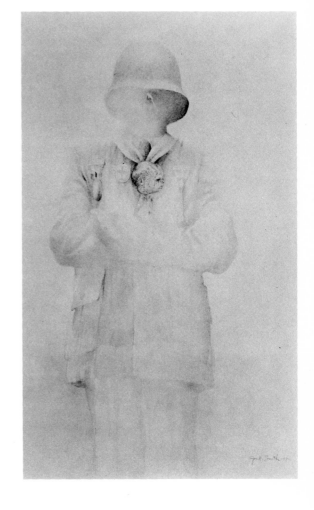

58 Advertising
Artist/**Randall McKissick**
Art Director/Randall McKissick

60 Institutional
Artist/**Fred Otnes**
Art Director/William Duevell & Henry Epstein
Client/ABC News

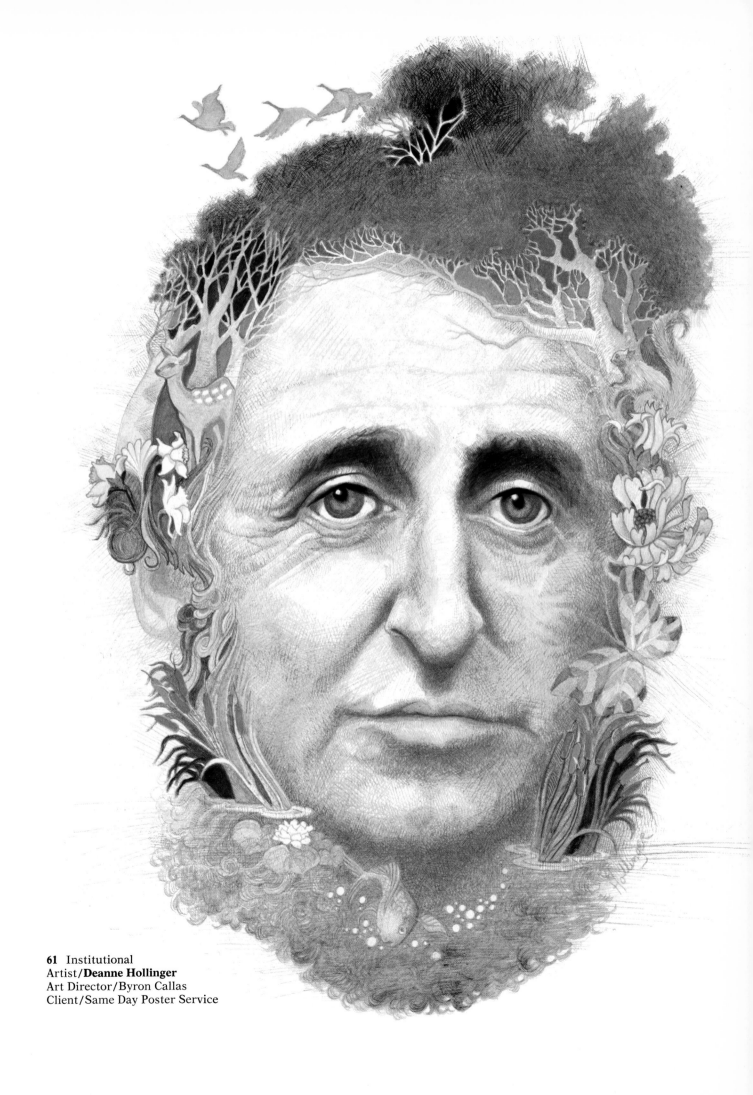

61 Institutional
Artist/**Deanne Hollinger**
Art Director/Byron Callas
Client/Same Day Poster Service

62 Editorial
Artist/**Donald M. Hedin**
Art Director/James Craig
Publication/American Artist Magazine

63 Advertising
Artist/**Wendell Minor**
Art Director/Joe Stelmach
Client/RCA Records

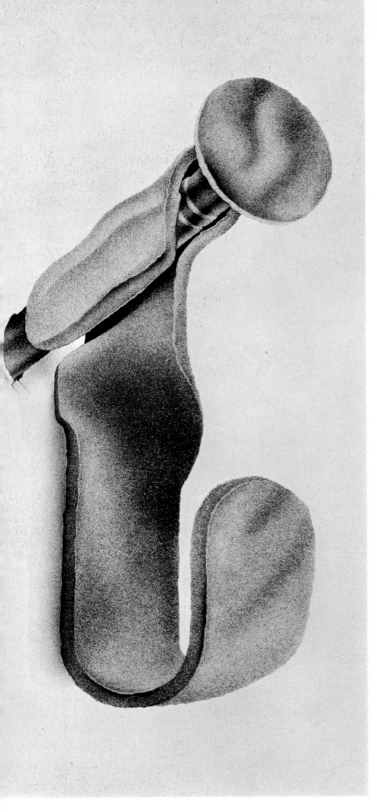

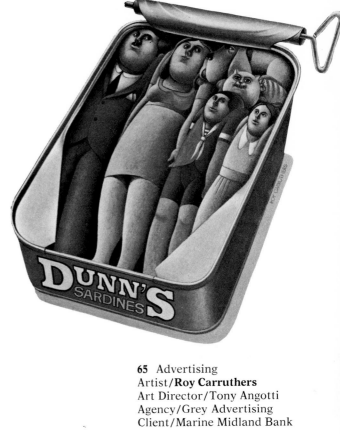

65 Advertising
Artist/**Roy Carruthers**
Art Director/Tony Angotti
Agency/Grey Advertising
Client/Marine Midland Bank

64 Advertising
Artist/**Argus Childers**
Art Director/Larry Pillot
Agency/Lang, Fisher, Stashower
Client/American Greeting Corp.

66 Editorial
Artist/**Don Almquist**
Art Director/Kirk Polking
Publication/Writer's Digest

67 Institutional
Artist/**Don Weller**
Art Director/Don Weller & Dennis Juett
Agency/Weller & Juett, Inc.
Client/Southern California Edison

68 Book
Artist/**Phil Berkman**
Art Director/Hal Kearney
Title/Accent
Publisher/Scott, Foresman & Co.

69 Advertising
Artist/**David Willardson**
Art Director/Ed Thrasher
Client/Warner Bros. Records

70 Advertising
Artist/**Dennis Corrigan**
Art Director/Acy Lehman
Client/RCA Records

71 Advertising
Artist/**John Ryan**
Art Director/John Ryan
Client/CBS Television

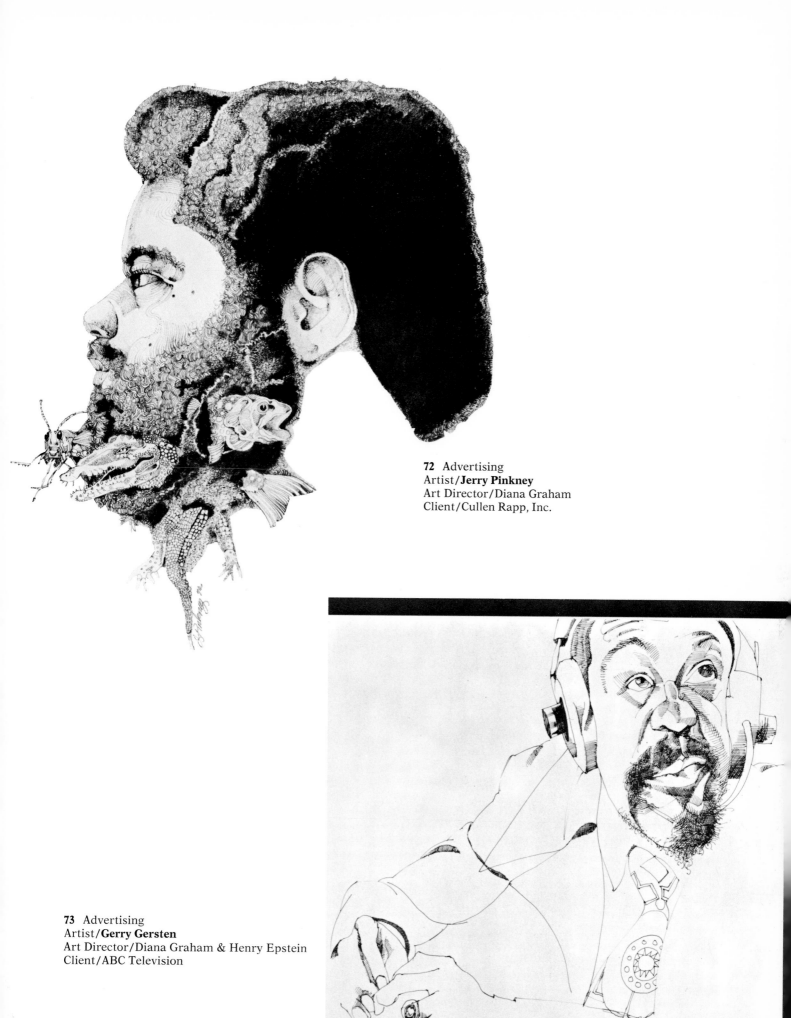

72 Advertising
Artist/**Jerry Pinkney**
Art Director/Diana Graham
Client/Cullen Rapp, Inc.

73 Advertising
Artist/**Gerry Gersten**
Art Director/Diana Graham & Henry Epstein
Client/ABC Television

74 Book
Artist/**Alex Ebel**
Art Director/Gordon Kwiatkowski
Title/Plants of Long Ago
Publisher/Field Enterprises Educational Corp.

75 Institutional
Artist/**Luther Travis**
Art Director/A. A. Versh
Client/Dorothy Simmons, Inc.

76 Book
Artist/**Luigi Castiglioni**
Art Director/Charles Volpe
Title/Invisible Horizons
Publisher/Ace Books

77 Book
Artist/**Monika Laimgruber**
Art Director/Gordon Kwiatkowski
Title/True Tales and Tall Tales
Publisher/Field Enterprises Education Corp.

78 Book
Artist/**Richard Amsel**
Art Director/Carol Inouye
Title/Nijinsky
Publisher/Pocket Books

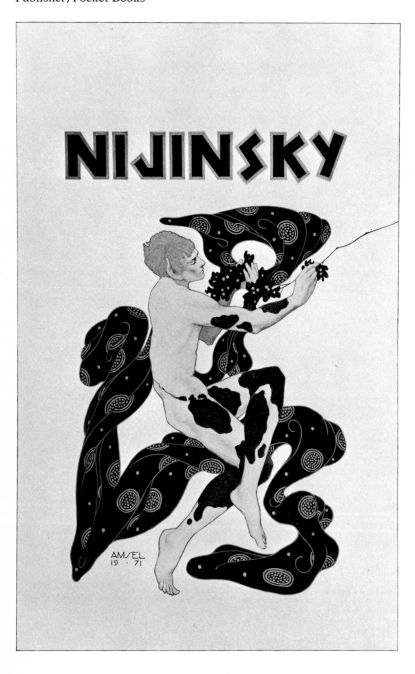

79 Institutional
Artist/**Walter Einsel**
Art Director/Charles Haber

81 Book
Artist/**Ted Lewin**
Art Director/John Van Zwienen
Title/Cool Cat
Publisher/Dell Publishing Co., Inc.

80 Editorial
Artist/**Hildy Maze**
Art Director/Hildy Maze
Publication/Audience Magazine

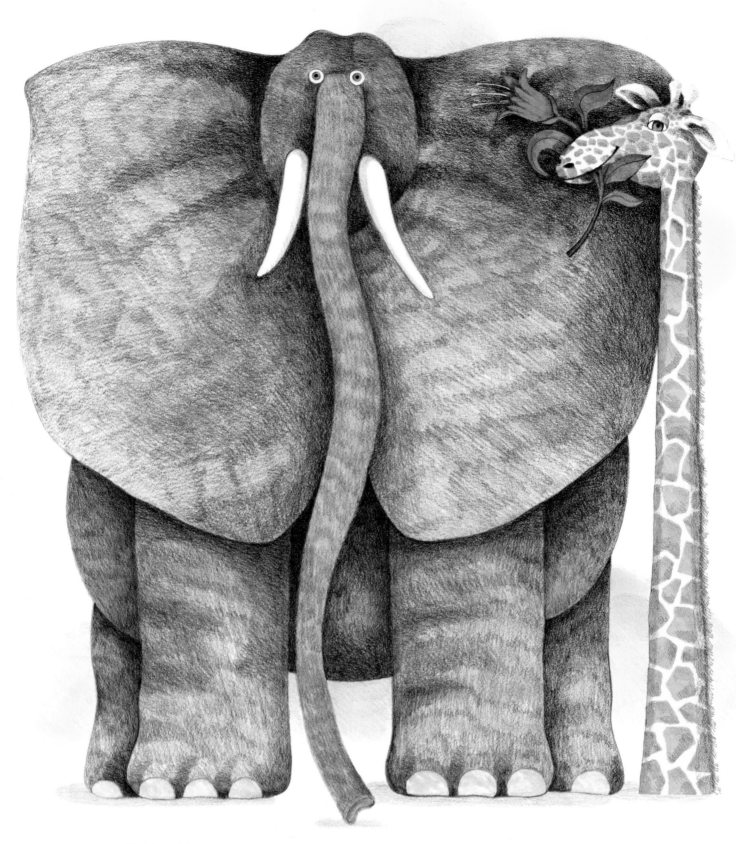

82 Advertising
Artist/**Gordon Kibbee**
Art Director/Frank Perry & Art Christy
Agency/Fuller & Smith & Ross, Inc.
Client/Mobil Oil Corp.

83 Editorial
Artist/**Philip Wende**
Art Director/Don Koontz
Publication/Georgia Magazine

84 Editorial
Artist/**Alex Gnidziejko**
Art Director/Arthur Paul & Kerig Pope
Publication/Playboy Magazine

85 Advertising
Artist/**Albert F. Michini**
Art Director/Albert F. Michini

86 Editorial
Artist/**Paul Giovanopoulos**
Art Director/Norman Schaefer
Publication/Intellectual Digest

87 Book
Artist/**Vincent Petragnani**
Art Director/Vincent Petragnani

88 Editorial
Artist/**Ted CoConis**
Art Director/Bernard White
Publication/Argosy Magazine

89 Book
Artist/**Tom Feelings**
Art Director/Victoria Gomez
Title/Black Pilgrimage
Publisher/Lothrop, Lee & Shepard Co.

90 Book
Artist/**John Burningham**
Art Director/Aileen Friedman
Title/Mr. Gumpy's Outing
Publisher/Holt, Rinehart & Winston, Inc.

91 Editorial
Artist/**Doug Johnson**
Art Director/Arthur Paul & Bob Post
Publication/Playboy Magazine

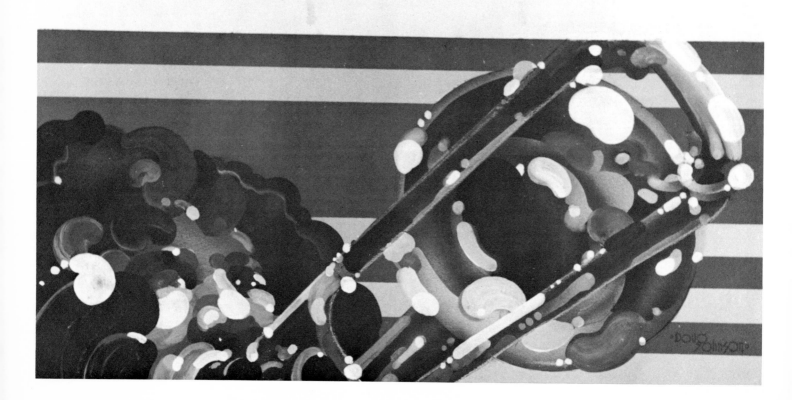

92 Institutional
Artist/**Allen M. Welkis**
Art Director/Allen M. Welkis

93 Book
Artist/**Beverly & Philip Wende**
Art Director/Beverly & Philip Wende

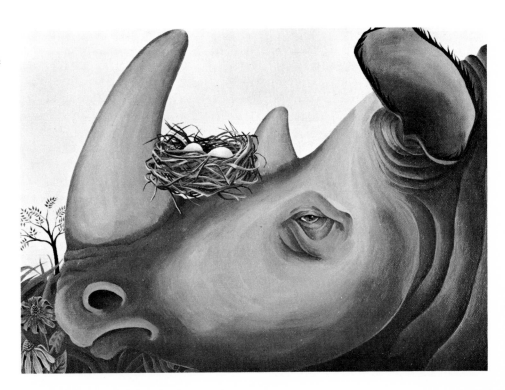

94 Book
Artist/**Etienne Delessert**
Title/Kipling Book
Publisher/Doubleday & Co., Inc.
■ **Gold Medal**

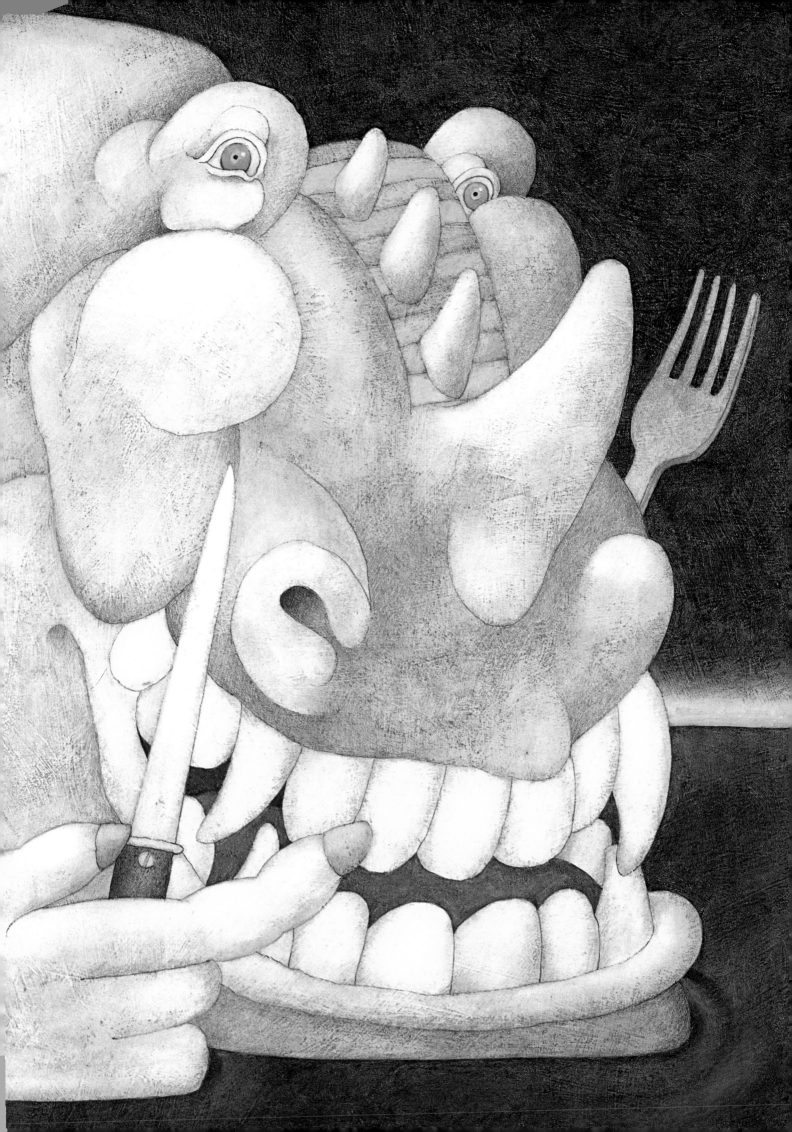

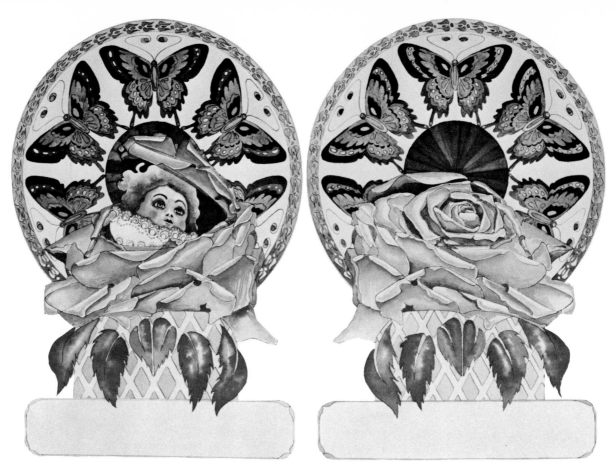

95 Book
Artist/**Susanne Valla**
Art Director/Susanne Valla

96 Editorial
Artist/**Mike Medow**
Art Director/Arthur Paul & Roy Moody
Publication/Playboy Magazine

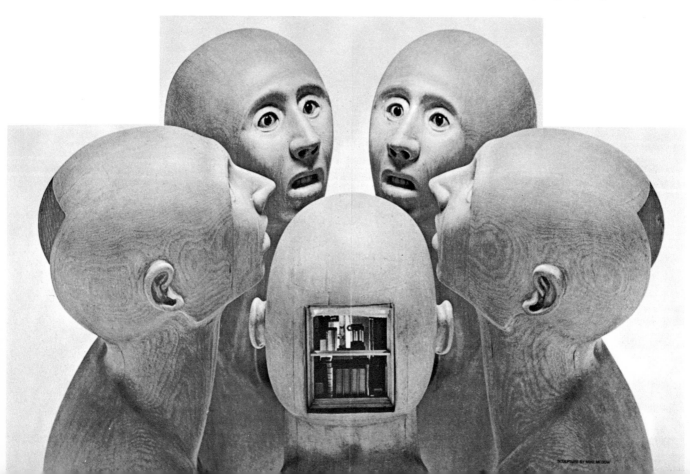

97 Editorial
Artist/**Edward Soyka**
Art Director/Norman Schaefer
Publication/Intellectual Digest

98 Book
Artist/**Leo Lionni**
Art Director/Janet Townsend
Title/Theodore
Publisher/Random House, Inc.

99 Editorial
Artist/**Ken Dallison**
Art Director/Gene Butera
Publication/Car and Driver Magazine

100 Book
Artist/**Nick Gaetano**
Art Director/Aileen Friedman
Title/Longhouse Winter
Publisher/Holt, Rinehart & Winston, Inc.

101 Book
Artist/**Robert K. Abbett**
Art Director/Peter Weed
Title/Greygallows
Publisher/Dodd, Mead & Co.

102 Advertising
Artist/**Alan Cober**
Art Director/Diana Graham
Client/Young Friends of City Center

103 Editorial
Artist/**Paul Calle**
Art Director/Paul Calle

104 Book
Artist/**Richard Bober**
Art Director/John Van Zwienen
Title/The Best of Friends
Publisher/Dell Publishing Co., Inc.

105 Institutional
Artist/**Cliff Condak**
Art Director/B. Martin Pedersen
Agency/Caldwell Communications
Client/American Airlines

106 Editorial
Artist/**Gerry Gersten**
Art Director/Al Greenberg
Publication/Family Health Magazine

107 Editorial
Artist/**Ronald Wolin**
Art Director/Mike Gaines
Publication/Pro Magazine

108 Institutional
Artist/**Dennis Anderson**
Art Director/Gary Britt
Agency/Dutch Hill Graphics

109 Book
Artist/**Roger Kastel**
Art Director/Leonard Leone
Title/The Metamorphosis
Publisher/Bantam Books, Inc.

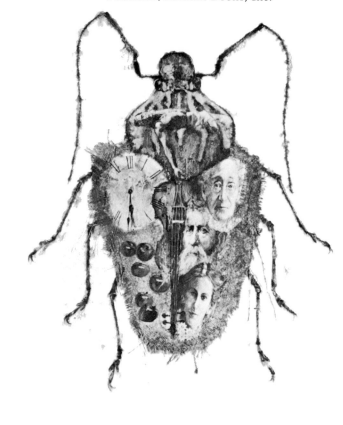

110 Advertising
Artist/**Richard Hess**
Art Director/Richard Hess
Agency/Richard Hess & Associates, Inc.
Client/Franklin Typographers

The Hare was once boasting of his speed before the other animals. "I have never yet been beaten," said he, "when I put forth my full speed. I challenge any one here to race with me."

The Tortoise said quietly: "I accept your challenge."

"This is a good joke," said the Hare; "I could dance around you all the way."

"Keep your boasting till you've beaten," answered the Tortoise. "Shall we race?"

So a course was fixed and a start was made. The Hare darted almost out of sight at once, but soon stopped and, to show his contempt for the Tortoise, lay down to have a nap. The Tortoise plodded on, and when the Hare awoke from his nap he saw the Tortoise just near the finish and could not run up in time to save the race.

The steady one can also win.
Aesop's Fables

111 Book
Artist/**Jim Crowell**
Art Director/Jim Crowell

112 Book
Artist/**Bob Jones**
Art Director/Bob Jones

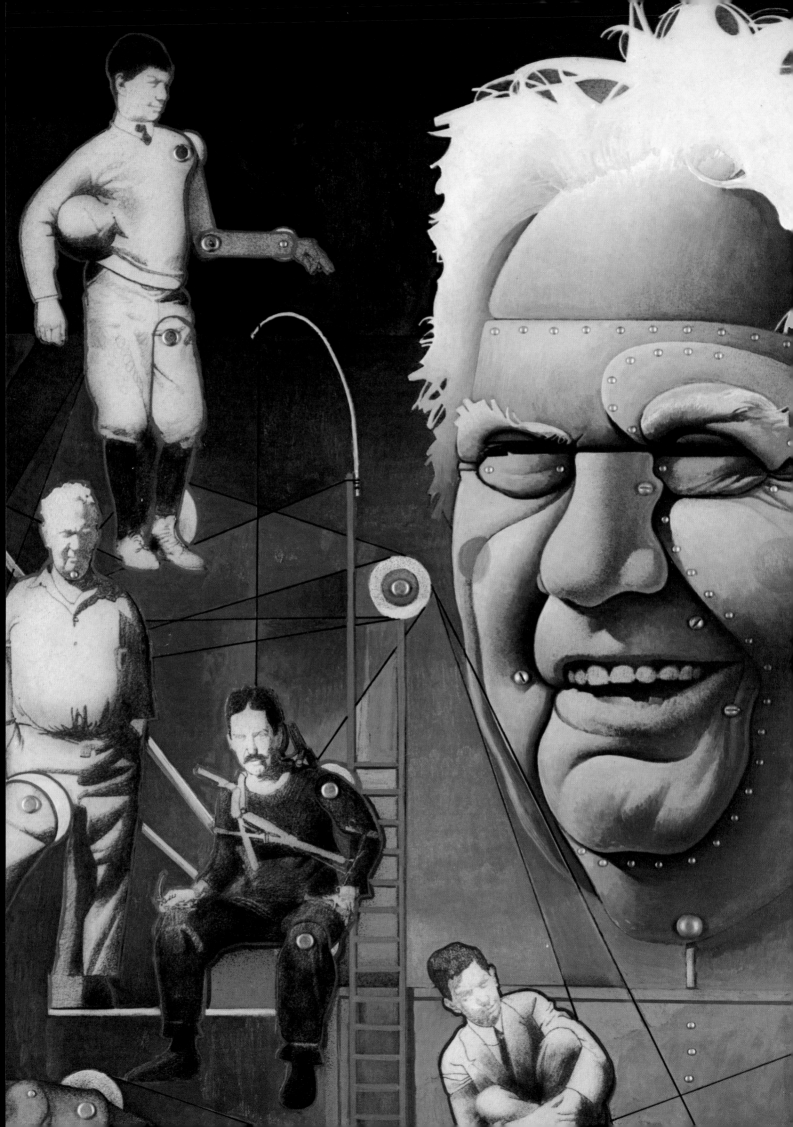

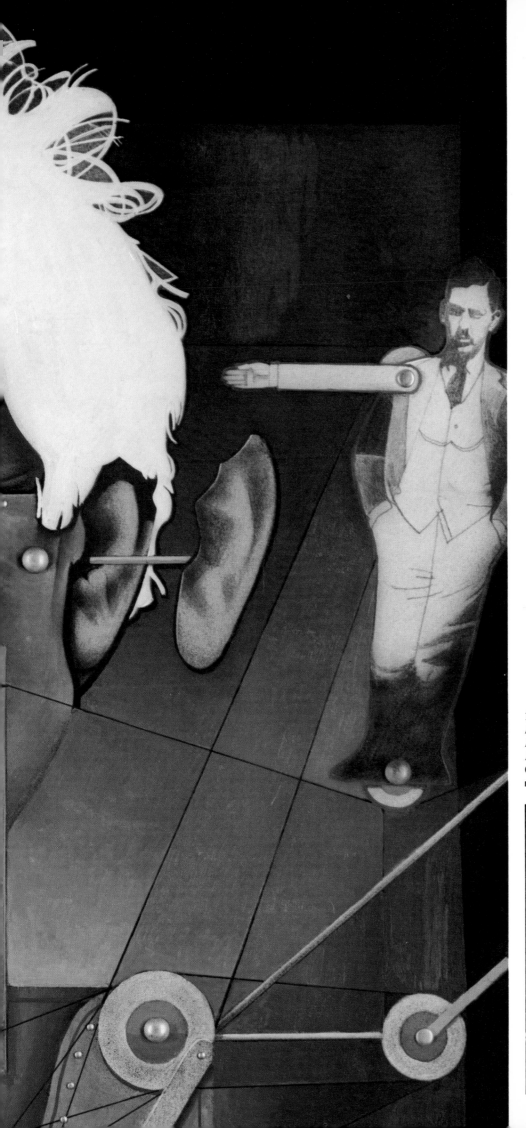

113 Institutional
Artist/**Mark English**
Art Director/Del Martin
Agency/Lord, Sullivan & Yoder Advertising
Client/Borden—Columbus Coated Fabrics
■ **Gold Medal**

114 Advertising
Artist/**James Barkley**
Art Director/Richard Bennett
Client/NBC Television

115 Advertising
Artist/**Ron Barry**
Art Director/Ron Barry
Agency/New Center Studios

116 Advertising
Artist/**Jackie L. W. Geyer**
Art Director/Ron Salter
Agency/Fahlgren & Associates
Client/Marbon Cycolac/Borg Warner Corp.

117 Advertising
Artist/**Raymond Ameijide**
Art Director/John Cavalieri & Robert Pearlman
Agency/Mixed Media
Client/Loews Hotels

118 Advertising
Artist/**George S. Gaadt**
Art Director/Ron Chory
Agency/Ketchum, MacLeod & Grove, Inc.
Client/Alcoa

119 Institutional
Artist/**James Spanfeller**
Art Director/James Spanfeller

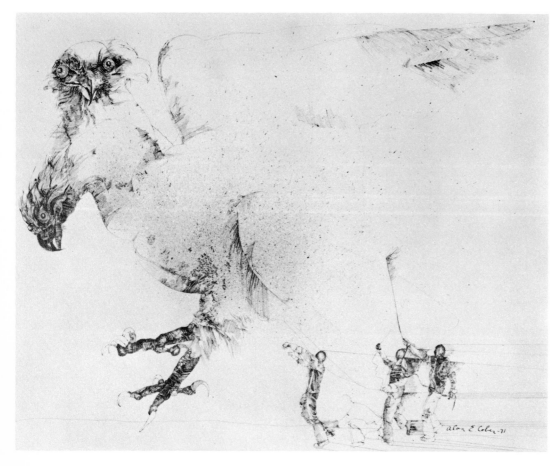

120 Editorial
Artist/**Alan Cober**
Art Director/Richard Gangel
Publication/Sports Illustrated

121 Advertising
Artist/**Jerry Dior**
Art Director/R. Downing & R. Gerstman
Agency/Gerstman & Myers
Client/Howard Johnson Co.

122 Book
Artist/**Shannon Stirnweis**
Art Director/David Glixson
Title/Ah! Wilderness
Publisher/Limited Editions

123 Book
Artist/**Milton Glaser**
Art Director/Alex Gotfryd
Title/Asimou's Annotated Don Juan
Publisher/Doubledav & Co., Inc.

124 Editorial
Artist/**Charles B. Slackman**
Art Director/Arthur Paul & Gordon Mortensen
Publication/Playboy Magazine

126 Editorial
Artist/**Ken Graning**
Art Director/Dick Cheverton

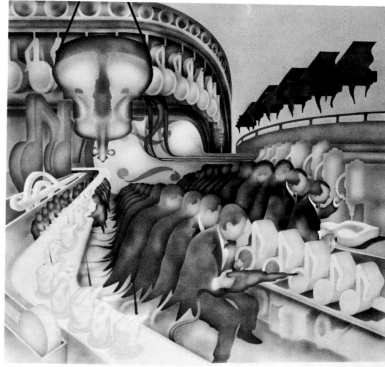

125 Book
Artist/**Donald M. Hedin**
Art Director/Walter Brooks
Publisher/Western Publishing Co., Inc.

127 Institutional
Artist/**Gennaro Trainello**
Art Director/Gennaro Trainello

LET'S
PUT THE
"A"
BACK
IN PEACE

129 Editorial
Artist/**Chuck Mitchell**
Art Director/James Craig
Publication/American Artist Magazine

128 Book
Artist/**Arvis Stewart**
Art Director/Aileen Friedman
Title/Winter Thing
Publisher/Holt, Rinehart & Winston, Inc.

130 Book
Artist/**Sal Murdocca**
Art Director/Sal Murdocca
Publisher/Holt, Rinehart & Winston, Inc.

131 Book
Artist/**Lorraine Fox**
Art Director/Lorraine Fox

132 Advertising
Artist/**Charles White III**
Art Director/Craig Braun
Agency/Wilkes & Braun, Inc.
Client/Ode Records

133 Institutional
Artist/**Lorraine Fox**
Art Director/Diana Graham
Agency/Cullen Rapp, Inc.

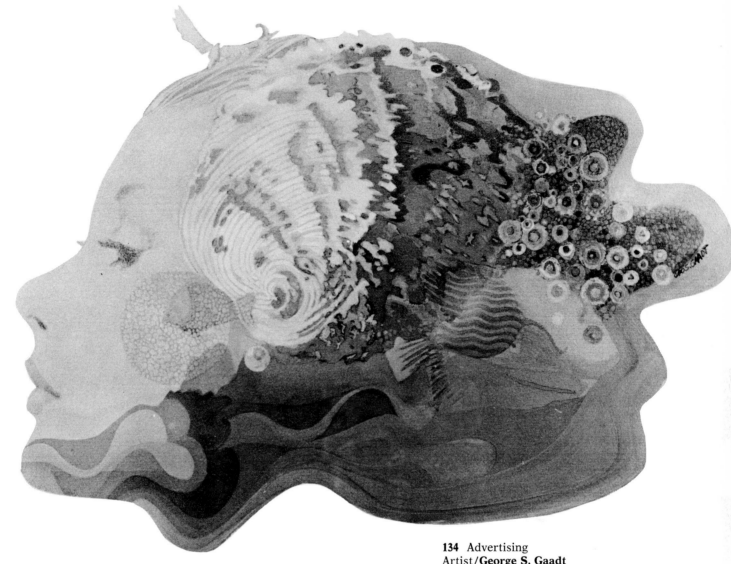

134 Advertising
Artist/**George S. Gaadt**
Art Director/Ron Chory
Agency/Ketchum, MacLeod & Grove, Inc.
Client/Alcoa

135 Advertising
Artist/**Bill Hofmann**
Art Director/Robert L. Heimall
Client/Elektra Records

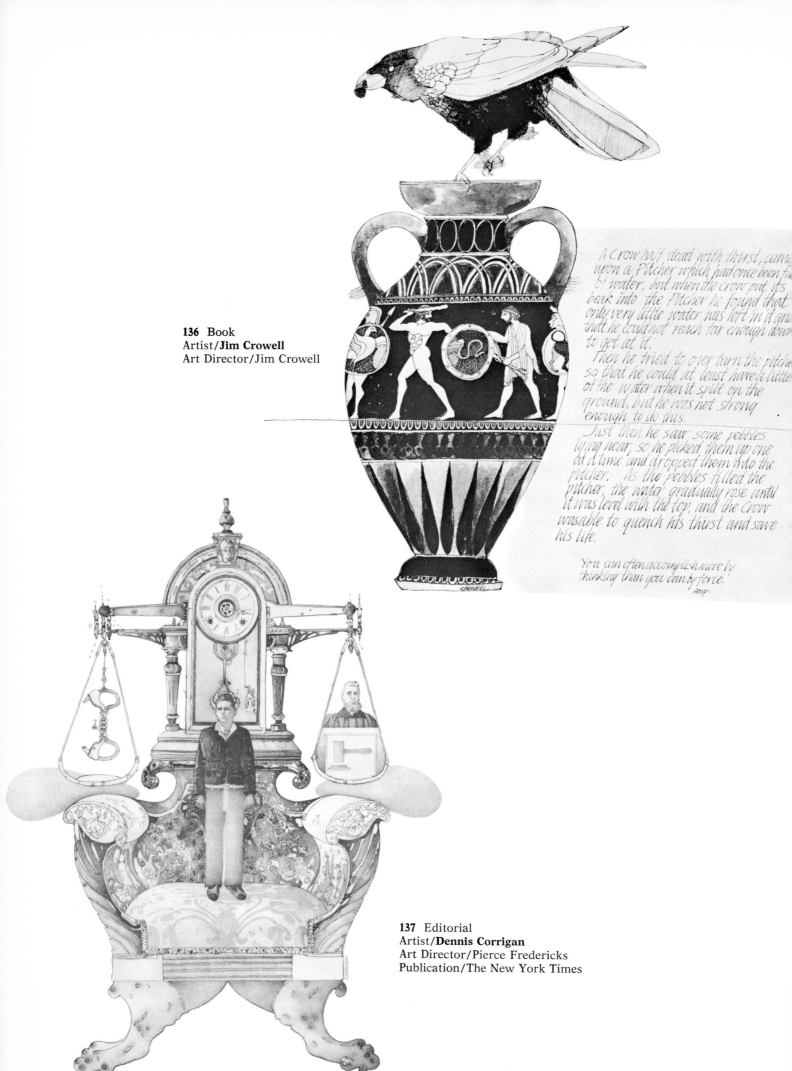

136 Book
Artist/**Jim Crowell**
Art Director/Jim Crowell

A Crow half dead with thirst, came
upon a Pitcher which had once been full
of water, but when the crow put its
beak into the Pitcher he found that
only very little water was left in it and
that he could not reach far enough down
to get at it.

Then he tried to overturn the pitcher
so that he could at least have a little
of the water when it spilt on the
ground, but he was not strong
enough to do this.

Just then he saw some pebbles
lying near, so he picked them up one
at a time and dropped them into the
pitcher. As the pebbles filled the
pitcher, the water gradually rose until
it was level with the top, and the Crow
was able to quench his thirst and save
his life.

You can often accomplish more by
thinking than you can by force.
Aesop

137 Editorial
Artist/**Dennis Corrigan**
Art Director/Pierce Fredericks
Publication/The New York Times

138 Book
Artist/**Fred Mason**
Art Director/Fred Mason

139 Editorial
Artist/**John Mardon**
Art Director/Max Newton
Publication/Weekend Magazine

140 Advertising
Artist/**Christine Duke**
Art Director/Christine Duke

141 Book
Artist/**Ken Perenyi**
Art Director/John Van Zwienen
Title/In the Country of Ourselves
Publisher/Dell Publishing Co., Inc.

142 Advertising
Artist/**Jack Unruh**
Art Director/Jerry McPhail
Agency/Bloom Advertising
Client/Howard Wolf

143 Book
Artist/**Alan Lee**
Art Director/Charles Volpe
Title/The Compleat Werewolf
Publisher/Ace Books

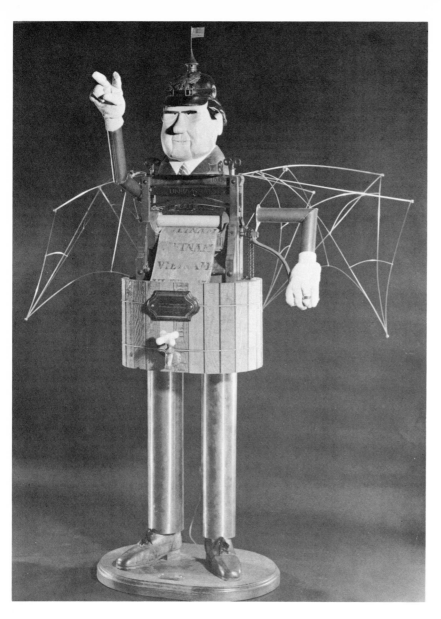

145 Book
Artist/**Jose Areugo & Ariane Areugo**
Art Director/Robert Kraus
Title/Milton the Early Riser
Publisher/Windmill Books, Inc. &
　　　　　　E.P. Dutton and Co., Inc.

144 Institutional
Artist/**Walter Einsel**
Art Director/Walter Einsel

146 Advertising
Artist/**Shelley Freshman**
Art Director/Shelley Freshman

147 Advertising
Artist/**Dick Anderson**
Art Director/Dick Anderson

148 Editorial
Artist/**Michael Eagle**
Art Director/Sal Lazzarotti
Publication/Guideposts Magazine

150 Institutional
Artist/**Mark English**
Art Director/Del Martin
Agency/Lord, Sullivan & Yoder Advertising
Client/Borden-Columbus Coated Fabrics

151 Advertising
Artist/**Richard Amsel**
Art Director/Craig Braun
Agency/Wilkes & Braun, Inc.
Client/Ode Records

149 Book
Artist/**Lew McCance**
Art Director/Tom Von Der Linn
Title/Maigrét
Publisher/Reader's Digest Association

152 Institutional
Artist/**Bob Prasciunas**
Art Director/Dick Anderson
Agency/Studio One, Inc.

153 Advertising
Artist/**Dick Anderson**
Art Director/Bob Prasciunas

154 Institutional
Artist/**Jerry McDaniel**
Art Director/Jerry McDaniel

155 Institutional
Artist/**Bart Forbes**
Art Director/Mike Gaines
Client/National Football League

156 Advertising
Artist/**Albert J. Pastore**
Art Director/Albert J. Pastore

157 Editorial
Artist/**Lemuel Line**
Art Director/Lemuel Line

158 Book
Artist/**Robert Andrew Parker**
Art Director/Jane Byers Bierhorst
Title/Zeek Silver Moon
Publisher/The Dial Press

159 Book
Artist/**Richard Brown**
Art Director/Will Winslow
Title/Even the Devil Is Afraid of a Shrew
Publisher/Addison-Wesley Publishing Co.

160 Editorial
Artist/**Louis G. Aronson**
Art Director/Jack Lund
Publication/Chicago Tribune Magazine

161 Book
Artist/**Tom Hall**
Art Director/Leonard Leone
Title/Mandy
Publisher/Bantam Books, Inc.

162 Book
Artist/**Tony Chen**
Art Director/Victoria Gomez
Title/Wart Hogs
Publisher/Lothrop, Lee & Sheppard Co., Inc.
■ **Award of Excellence**

163 Book
Artist/**Don Brautigam**
Art Director/Greg Wozney
Title/The Other Dimension
Publisher/Scholastic Books

164 Editorial
Artist/**George Roth**
Art Director/Arthur Paul & Kerig Pope
Publication/Playboy Magazine

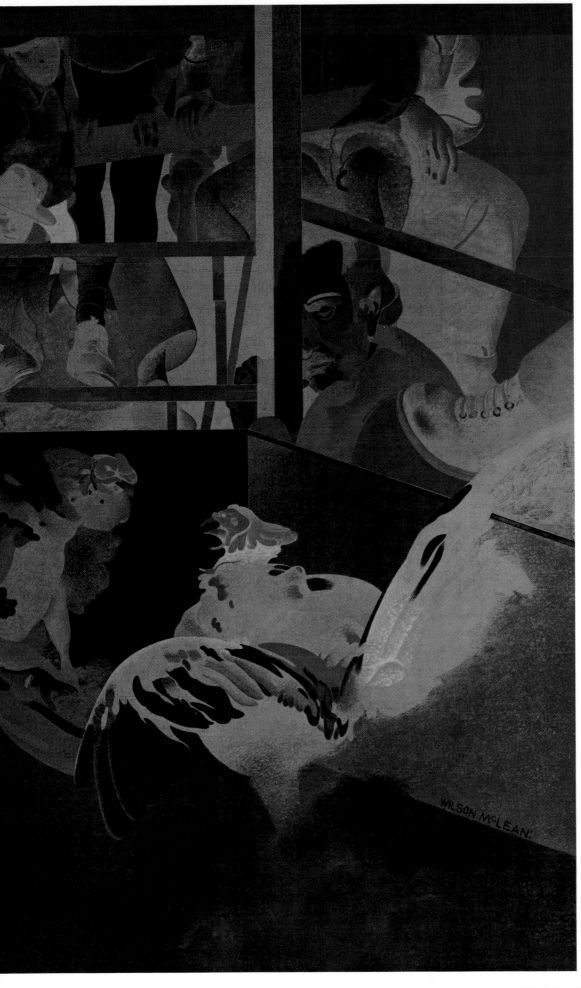

165 Editorial
Artist/**Wilson McLean**
Art Director/Richard Gangel
Publication/Sports Illustrated
■ **Award of Excellence**

166 Editorial
Artist/**Robert LoGrippo**
Art Director/William F. Cadge
Publication/Redbook Magazine

167 Editorial
Artist/**John Berkey**
Art Director/John Berkey

168 Editorial
Artist/**Dick Brown**
Art Director/Dick Brown

169 Institutional
Artist/**John Alcorn**
Art Director/Lou Dorfsman
Client/CBS Stations

170 Editorial
Artist/**Bernie Fuchs**
Art Director/William F. Cadge
Publication/Redbook Magazine
■ **Award of Excellence**

171 Advertising
Artist/**Robert Cunningham**
Art Director/Robert Cunningham

172 Book
Artist/**Robert LoGrippo**
Art Director/Robert LoGrippo

173 Editorial
Artist/**John Berkey**
Art Director/John Berkey

174 Editorial
Artist/**Paul Melia**
Art Director/Paul Melia

175 Editorial
Artist/**Deanna Glad**
Art Director/Elin Waite
Publication/Westways Magazine

176 Editorial
Artist/**Ronald Wolin**
Art Director/Mike Gaines
Publication/Pro Magazine

177 Book
Artist/**John Berkey**
Art Director/Bob Blanchard
Title/Star #6
Publisher/Ballantine Books, Inc.

ORIGINAL 95¢

STAR 6
SCIENCE FICTION
Edited by Frederik Pohl

STAR 6

Ballantine Books Science Fiction 02722·1·095

Edited by Frederik Pohl

345-02722-1-095

178 Institutional
Artist/**Donni Giambrone**
Art Director/Bill Cunningham
Client/Hallmark Cards, Inc.

179 Institutional
Artist/**Bruce Macdonald**
Art Director/Bruce Macdonald

181 Book
Artist/**Tony Chen**
Art Director/Victoria Gomez
Title/Run, Zebra Run
Publisher/Lothrop, Lee & Shepard Co., Inc.

180 Institutional
Artist/**John Freas**
Art Director/Alan Klawans
Agency/Smith, Kline & French
Client/Smith, Kline & French

182 Book
Artist/**Gordon Kibbee**
Art Director/Annika Umans
Title/The Jest of Haha-Laba
Publisher/Houghton Mifflin Co.

184 Advertising
Artist/**Jim Manos**
Art Director/Paula Bisacca
Agency/Album Graphics, Inc.
Client/Atlantic Records

183 Editorial
Artist/**Bob Post**
Art Director/Arthur Paul & Bob Post
Publication/Playboy Magazine

185 Institutional
Artist/**David Willardson**
Art Director/David Willardson

186 Advertising
Artist/**David Plourde**
Art Director/Jim McFarland
Agency/Sudler & Hennessey, Inc.
Client/Parke-Davis

187 Advertising
Artist/**David Willardson**
Art Director/Chris Brown
Agency/Honig-Cooper & Harrington
Client/Levi-Strauss

188 Advertising
Artist/**David M. Gaadt**
Art Director/Dan Scarlotto
Agency/Cargill, Wilson & Acree, Inc.
Client/Colonial Bread Co.

189 Advertising
Artist/**Henry Kolodziej**
Art Director/Gary Shortt
Agency/McNamara Associates
Client/Michigan State Fair

190 Advertising
Artist/**Richard Amsel**
Art Director/Talivaldis Stubis
Agency/Bill Gold Advertising, Inc.
Client/National General Pictures

191 Book
Artist/**Martin & Alice Provensen**
Art Director/Robert D. Scudellari
Title/Play on Words
Publisher/Random House, Inc.

192 Book
Artist/**Patric Fourshe**
Art Director/Patric Fourshé

193 Advertising
Artist/**Janet McCaffery**
Art Director/Walter Kaprielian & Peter Welsch
Agency/Ketchum, MacLeod & Grove, Inc.
Client/Newark District Ford Dealers

JH 9506

195 Institutional
Artist/**Ruth Strosser**
Art Director/Ruth Strosser
Client/Pitt Studios

194 Institutional
Artist/**David Kilmer**
Art Director/Allen Porter
Agency/Porter, Goodman & Cheatham
Client/Testor Corp.

196 Advertising
Artist/**D. R. Shuck**
Art Director/D. R. Shuck

197 Editorial
Artist/**Richard Huebner**
Art Director/Richard Huebner

198 Editorial
Artist/**Ken Dallison**
Art Director/Gene Butera
Publication/Car and Driver Magazine

199 Editorial
Artist/**Alan Cober**
Art Director/Richard Gangel
Publication/Sports Illustrated

200 Editorial
Artist/**Wilson McLean**
Art Director/Forbes Lloyd Linkhorn
Publication/American Journal of Nursing

201 Book
Artist/**Bill Chambers**
Art Director/Bill Chambers

202 Editorial
Artist/**Richard Amsel**
Art Director/Herbert Bleiweiss & Bruce Danbrot
Publication/Ladies' Home Journal

203 Editorial
Artist/**Etienne Delessert**
Art Director/Modesto Torre
Publication/McCall's Magazine

The Earring

204 Institutional
Artist/**James Barkley**
Art Director/James Barkley
Client/Our Own Little Studio

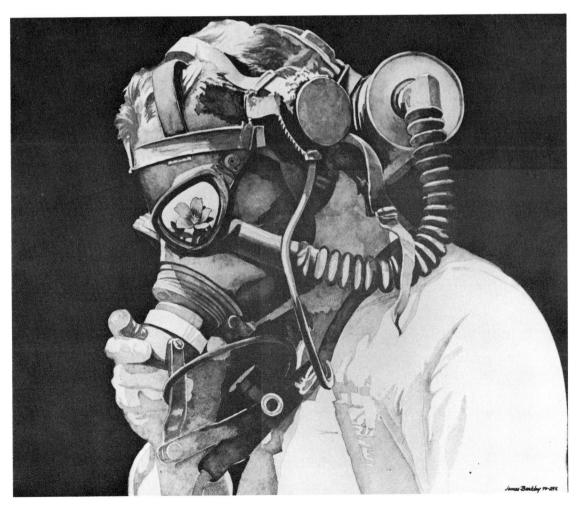

205 Institutional
Artist/**Bernard L. D'Andrea**
Art Director/Bernard L. D'Andrea

206 Advertising
Artist/**Alex Gnidziejko**
Art Director/Joe Stelmach
Client/RCA Records

207 Editorial
Artist/**Roy Carruthers**
Art Director/Arthur Paul
Publication/Playboy Magazine

208 Institutional
Artist/**Gerry Gersten**
Art Director/Gerry Gersten

210 Editorial
Artist/**Peter Copeland**
Art Director/Emma Landau
Publication/American Heritage Magazine

209 Advertising
Artist/**David M. Gaadt**
Art Director/Dick Henderson
Agency/Cole, Henderson, Drake, Inc.
Client/Aviation Insurance Agency

211 Editorial
Artist/**Peter Copeland**
Art Director/Emma Landau
Publication/American Heritage Magazine

212 Advertising
Artist/**Dick Anderson**
Art Director/Larry Waxberg
Agency/Needham, Harper, Steers
Client/ITT

213 Book
Artist/**Ann Lee Polus**
Art Director/Ann Lee Polus
Title/The Continuing Adventures of Isabel
Publisher/David M. Pesanelli, Inc.

214 Editorial
Artist/**Dennis Luczak**
Art Director/John Temple
Publication/Tuesday

215 Editorial
Artist/**Daniel Schwartz**
Art Director/Herbert Bleiweiss
Publication/Ladies' Home Journal

216 Book
Artist/**James Spanfeller**
Art Director/Harriett Barton
Publisher/Atheneum Publishers

217 Institutional
Artist/**Marvin Mattelson**
Art Director/Stanley Church
Client/LEASCO Corp.

218 Advertising
Artist/**Robert Peak**
Art Director/Kenneth Krom
Agency/Leo Burnett Co.
Client/Philip Morris Inc.

219 Advertising
Artist/**Howard Terpning**
Art Director/Jack Marinelli
Client/Winchester-Western

220 Advertising
Artist/**Ted CoConis**
Art Director/George Estes
Client/RCA Records

221 Institutional
Artist/**Anthony C. Russo**
Art Director/Anthony C. Russo

222 Advertising
Artist/**Tom Wilson**
Art Director/Tom Wilson
Client/American Greetings Corp.

223 Editorial
Artist/**Richard Corson**
Art Director/William A. Motta
Publication/Road & Track

224 Institutional
Artist/**Anthony C. Russo**
Art Director/Anthony C. Russo

226 Editorial
Artist/**Edward Sorel**
Art Director/Richard Hess
Publication/Vista Magazine

225 Book
Artist/**Ken Riley**
Art Director/Leonard Leone
Title/The Night Thoreau Spent in Jail
Publisher/Bantam Books, Inc.

227 Book
Artist/**Bob Jones**
Art Director/Bob Jones

228 Book
Artist/**Barbara Bascove**
Art Director/Annika Umans
Title/Tomorrow, Tomorrow, Tomorrow
Publisher/Houghton Mifflin Co.

229 Editorial
Artist/**Richard Sparks**
Art Director/Wim Vogues
Publication/Nieuwe Reyu

STANLEY KUBRICK'S
CLOCKWORK ORANGE

230 Advertising
Artist/**Philip Castle**
Art Director/Bill Gold
Agency/Bill Gold Advertising, Inc.
Client/Warner Bros. Pictures

231 Advertising
Artist/**Philip Wende**
Art Director/Bob Pitt
Agency/Burton Campbell Kelly
Client/Peoples

232 Book
Artist/**Reginald Pollack**
Art Director/James K. Davis
Title/Seneca's Oedipus
Publisher/Doubleday & Co., Inc.

233 Institutional
Artist/**Ron Carreiro**
Art Director/Paul Beaulieu
Client/Media Concepts

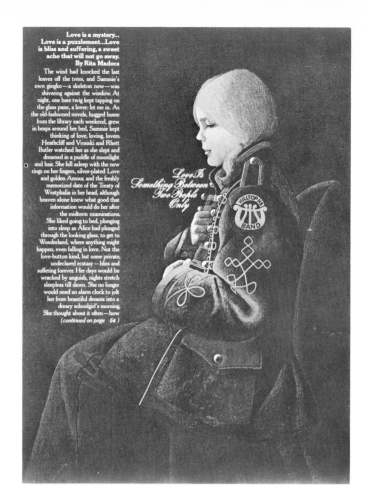

234 Editorial
Artist/**Chuck Wilkenson**
Art Director/Herbert Bleiweiss & Bruce Danbrot
Publication/Ladies' Home Journal

235 Advertising
Artist/**Roy Andersen**
Art Director/Ted Gall
Agency/Jack O'Grady Studios

236 Book
Artist/**Nick Gaetano**
Art Director/Susan Mann
Title/Longhouse Winter
Publisher/Holt, Rinehart & Winston, Inc.

238 Book
Artist/**John Burningham**
Art Director/Aileen Friedman
Title/Mr. Gumpy's Outing
Publisher/Holt, Rinehart & Winston, Inc.

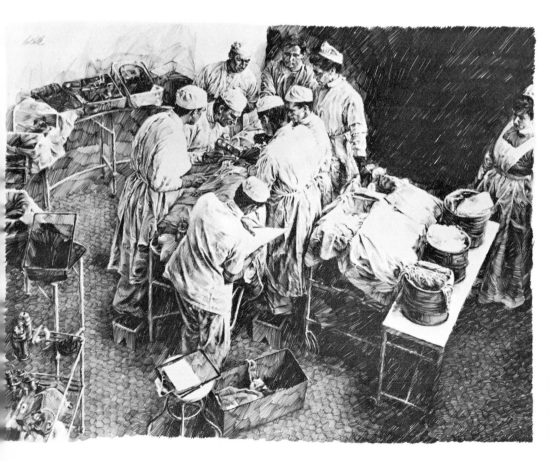

237 Advertising
Artist/**Paul Calle**
Art Director/Roger Core
Agency/Medicus
Client/Schering Corp.

240 Book
Artist/**Lester Abrams**
Art Director/Susan Mann
Title/The Four Donkeys
Publisher/Holt, Rinehart & Winston, Inc.

Thinking the Baker's manners were even lumpier than his cheesecakes, the Tailor stitched away as fast as he could. "Oh, that horrible jacket! Oh dear, oh dear," he muttered to his pet otter. "I hate the very sight of it! True, I made the thing for him in the first place. But only because he'd have it no other way. The fellow's baking is bad enough, but his taste in clothing is worse!"

At last rid of the Baker and his hideous jacket, the Tailor packed up his bolts of cloth, shears, and iron. Shouldering the bundle, he hurried out of the shop and started off on the road to the fair.

239 Book
Artist/**Gerald McConnell**
Art Director/Gerald McConnell

Faster than Stuart, more decisively than Stonewall Jackson, the blight swept the ridges clean.

Shenandoah National Park

Despite his burden, the Tailor went along quickly, wondering all the while how he would spend the profits he was sure would soon line his pockets.

"A new ironing board? A new cutting table? A new kitchen stove for my wife?"

The Tailor snapped his fingers. "No! Best yet, a way to have all and more. A signboard to hang outside my shop!

"Just so," he chattered on. "The biggest, brightest signboard, and my name in the boldest lettering. That's bound to draw more customers. I'll have all the fashionable folk at my door, even the Mayor himself!"

242 Book
Artist/**Gilbert Stone**
Art Director/Carol Inouye
Title/Crime & Punishment
Publisher/Pocket Books

241 Advertising
Artist/**Raymond Ameijide**
Art Director/Richard Lockwood
Agency/Richard Lockwood, Inc.
Client/First National City Bank

243 Advertising
Artist/**Ted CoConis**
Art Director/Donald Smolen
Client/United Artists Corp.

244 Advertising
Artist/**Robert A. Heindel**
Art Director/Jack Marinelli
Agency/Leisure Marketing
Client/Winchester-Western

245 Advertising
Artist/**Raymond Ameijide**
Art Director/Glenn P. Kipp
Client/New Jersey Bell Telephone Co.

246 Editorial
Artist/**Jean Michel Folon**
Art Director/Alvin Grossman
Publication/McCall's Magazine

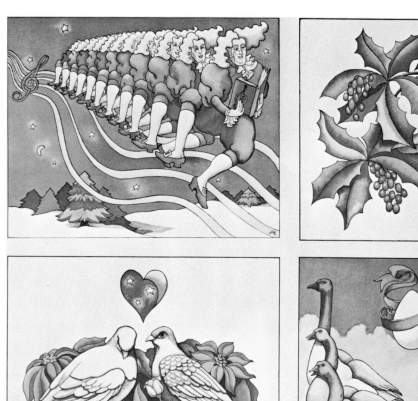

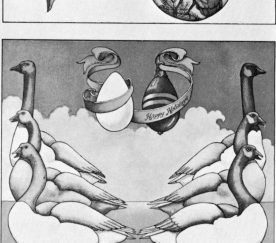

247 Advertising
Artist/**Jacqui Morgan**
Art Director/Greg Wozney
Client/Scholastic Magazines & Book Services, I

248 Editorial
Artist/**Vin Giuliani**
Art Director/Arthur Paul
Publication/Playboy Magazine

249 Editorial
Artist/**Bernie Fuchs**
Art Director/Al Barkow
Publication/Golf Magazine

250 Advertising
Artist/**Dennis Lyall**
Art Director/Jerry McPhail
Agency/The Bloom Agency
Client/Howard Wolf

251 Editorial
Artist/**Gervasio Gallardo**
Art Director/Joan Fenton
Publication/Seventeen Magazine

252 Book
Artist/**Bob McGinnis**
Art Director/Barbara Bertoli
Title/The Awakening
Publisher/Avon Books

253 Institutional
Artist/**Robert T. Handville**
Art Director/Stevan Dohanos
Client/National Park Service

254 Editorial
Artist/**Daniel Schwartz**
Art Director/William F. Cadge
Publication/Redbook Magazine

255 Institutional
Artist/**Robert Fillie**
Art Director/Robert Fillie

256 Editorial
Artist/**Allan Mardon**
Art Director/Arnold Hoffman
Publication/The New York Times

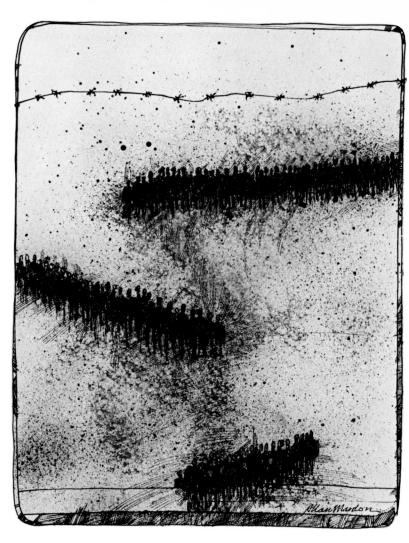

257 Book
Artist/**Jerry Pinkney**
Art Director/Madeline Wickham
Title/The Tiger, the Braham and the Jackal
Publisher/D. C. Heath & Co.

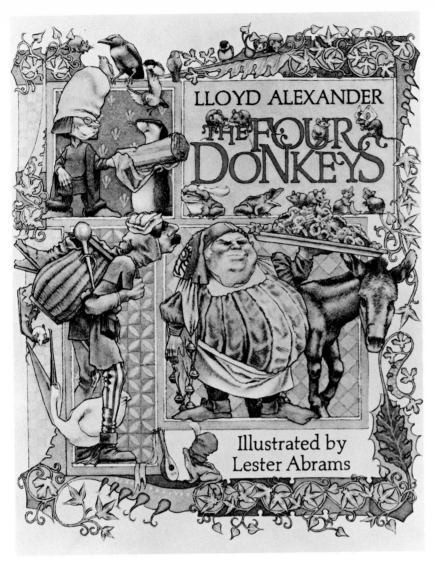

258 Book
Artist/**Lester Abrams**
Art Director/Susan Mann
Title/The Four Donkeys
Publisher/Holt, Rinehart & Winston, Inc.

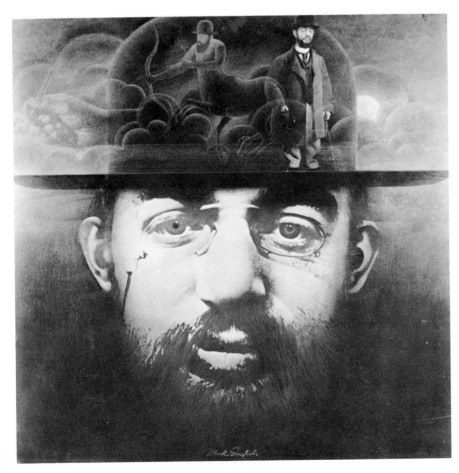

259 Institutional
Artist/**Mark English**
Art Director/Del Martin
Agency/Lord, Sullivan & Yoder Advertising
Client/Borden-Columbus Coated Fabrics

AO-51 $2.95

THE WORD IS HERE

Edited by
Keorapetse
Kgositsile

Poetry from
Modern Africa

260 Book
Artist/**Avel de Knight**
Art Director/Diana Klemin
Title/The Word is Here
Publisher/Doubleday & Co., Inc.

261 Advertising
Artist/**Howard Rogers**
Art Director/Alan Gorelick
Agency/Cummins, MacFail & Nutry, Inc.
Client/Johnson & Johnson (Athletic Div.)

Johnson & Johnson
Athletic Division
Product Information

262 Editorial
Artist/**Stanley Meltzoff**
Art Director/Richard Gangel
Publication/Sports Illustrated

263 Book
Artist/**Lois Darling**
Art Director/Cynthia Basil
Title/Worms (Nereid)
Publisher/William Morrow & Co., Inc.

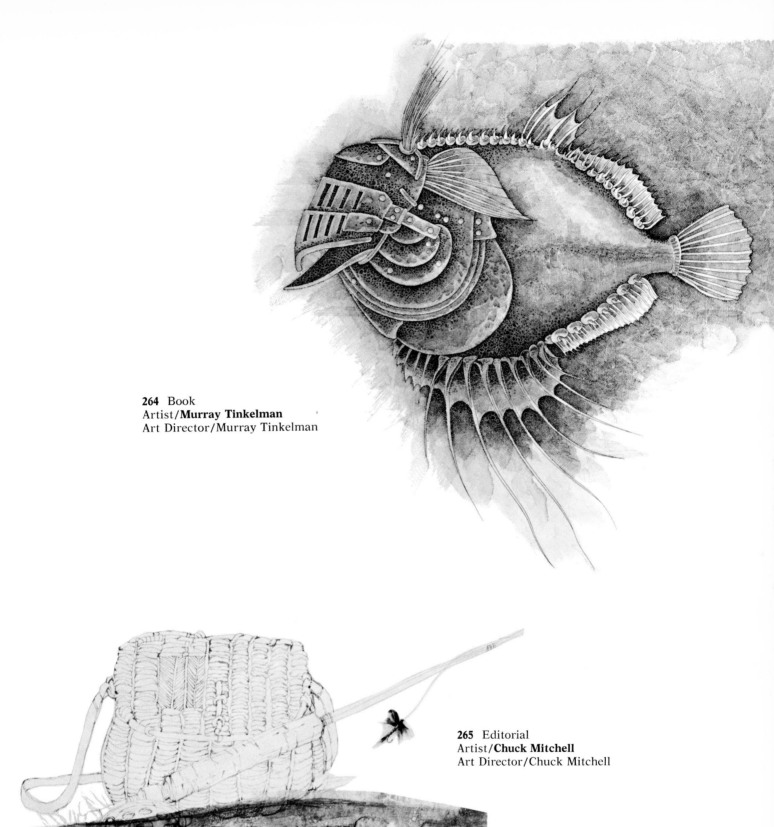

264 Book
Artist/**Murray Tinkelman**
Art Director/Murray Tinkelman

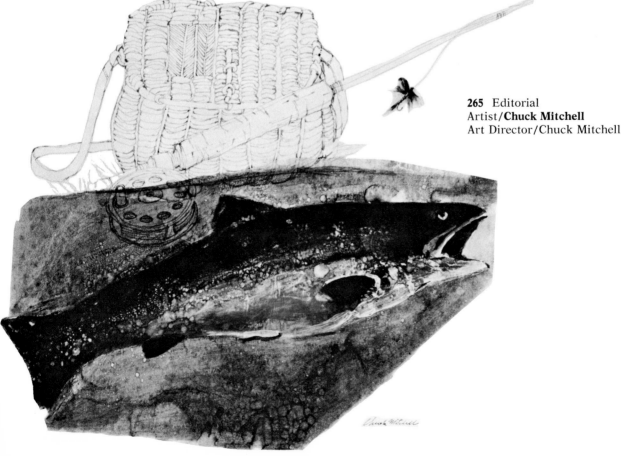

265 Editorial
Artist/**Chuck Mitchell**
Art Director/Chuck Mitchell

266 Editorial
Artist/**Mark English**
Art Director/William F. Cadge
Publication/Redbook Magazine
■ **Gold Medal**

267 Editorial
Artist/**Gene Calogero**
Art Director/Ted Blake
Publication/Scholastic Newstime

268 Book
Artist/**Marty Norman**
Art Director/Marty Norman

269 Book
Artist/**Ken Rinciari**
Art Director/Peggy Greenfield
Title/Anna Lisa's Nose
Publisher/Houghton Mifflin Co.

270 Book
Artist/**Alex Ebel**
Art Director/Gordon Kwiatkowski
Title/The Forests That Turned To Coal
Publisher/Field Enterprises Educational Corp.

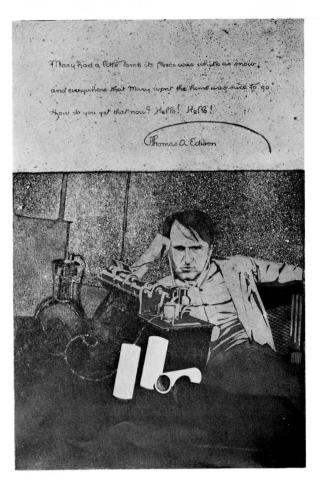

271 Book
Artist/**Salvatore Catalano**
Art Director/Greg Wozney
Title/The Second Coming
Publisher/Scholastic Books

272 Book
Artist/**Bill Chambers**
Art Director/Bill Chambers

273 Book
Artist/**Jose Aruego & Ariane Aruego**
Art Director/Robert Kraus
Title/Milton the Early Riser
Publisher/Windmill Books, Inc. &
               E.P. Dutton and Co., Inc.

274 Advertising
Artist/**John Ryan**
Art Director/John Ryan
Client/CBS Television

275 Editorial
Artist/**Nick Aristovulos**
Art Director/Joan Fenton
Publication/Seventeen Magazine

276 Editorial
Artist/**Don Weller**
Art Director/Hiroshi Ochi
Publication/Idea Magazine

277 Advertising
Artist/**John Sovjani**
Art Director/Murlin Marsh & Eugene Kolomatsky
Client/NBC Television

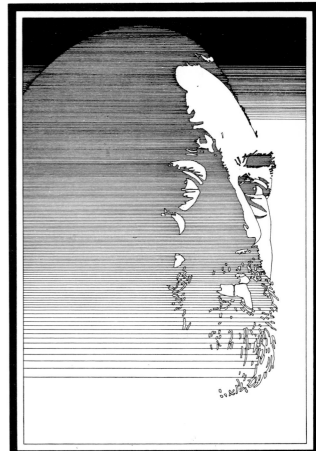

278 Book
Artist/**Eldon P. Slick**
Art Director/Don Fujimoto
Title/Drugs and Human Behavior
Publisher/CRM Books

279 Advertising
Artist/**Peter Schaumann**
Art Director/Robert L. Heimall
Client/Elektra Records

280 Book
Artist/**Ray Cruz**
Art Director/James K. Davis
Title/The Electric Radish
Publisher/Doubleday & Co., Inc.

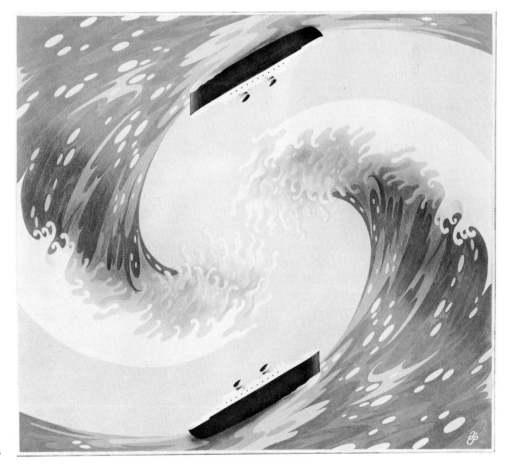

281 Advertising
Artist/**Don Ivan Punchatz**
Art Director/Ed Thrasher
Client/Warner Bros. Records

282 Editorial
Artist/**Robert J. Meganck**
Art Director/Robert J. Meganck
Publication/1972 P.G.A. Annual

283 Advertising
Artist/**David Wilcox**
Art Director/George Estes
Client/RCA Records

284 Book
Artist/**Nick Aristovulos**
Art Director/John Van Zwienen
Title/Player Piano
Publisher/Dell Publishing Co., Inc.

285 Institutional
Artist/**Bunny Carter**
Art Director/Jerry Sanders & Ben White
Agency/Sanders & White
Client/The Thalians

286 Advertising
Artist/**Bill Ressler**
Art Director/Al Smagala
Client/John Wanamaker

287 Institutional
Artist/**Harry J. Schaare**
Art Director/Harry J. Schaare

288 Institutional
Artist/**Dennis Anderson**
Art Director/Noel Gordon
Client/Hallmark Cards

289 Editorial
Artist/**John D. Dawson**
Art Director/Tom Gould
Publication/Psychology Today

290 Editorial
Artist/**Murray Tinkelman**
Art Director/Robert Hallock
Publication/Lithopinion

291 Institutional
Artist/**Wally Neibart**
Art Director/Wally Neibart
Agency/Ford/Byrne/Brennan
Client/INA

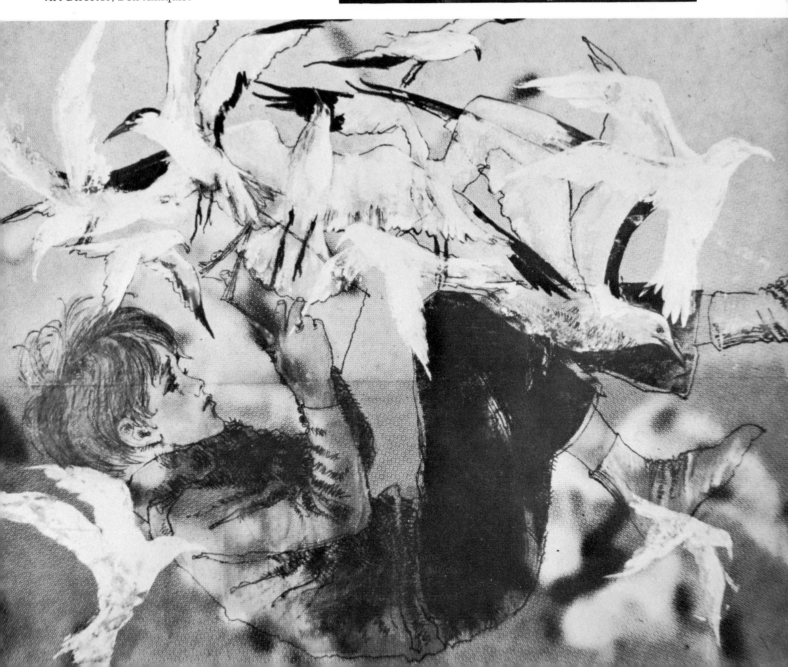

294 Editorial
Artist/**Etienne Delessert**
Art Director/Arthur Paul & Bob Post
Publication/Playboy

295 Advertising
Artist/**Robert J. Lee**
Art Director/Robert J. Lee

296 Book
Artist/**Nick Gaetano**
Art Director/Aileen Friedman
Title/Longhouse Winter
Publisher/Holt, Rinehart & Winston, Inc.

297 Editorial
Artist/**Murray Tinkelman**
Art Director/Robert Hallock
Publication/Lithopinion

298 Institutional
Artist/**Christine Duke**
Art Director/Christine Duke

299 Editorial
Artist/**Murray Tinkelman**
Art Director/Robert Hallock
Publication/Lithopinion

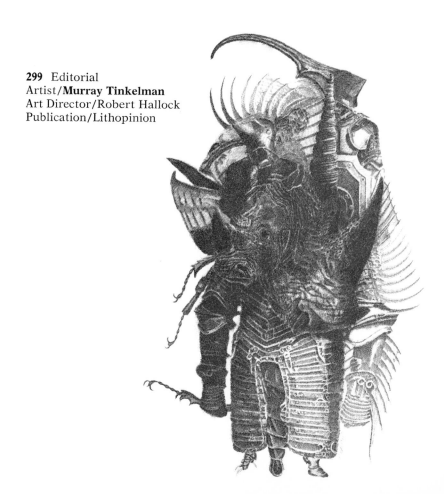

300 Institutional
Artist/**Paul Giovanopoulos**
Art Director/Paul Giovanopoulos
Client/Annette Kossen

301 Book
Artist/**Fred Thomas**
Art Director/Fred Thomas

302 Advertising
Artist/**Jackie L. W. Geyer & George S. Gaadt**
Art Director/Len Moser
Agency/Marini, Climes & Guip, Inc.
Client/U.S. Steel (Plastics Division)

303 Editorial
Artist/**Bill Charmatz**
Art Director/Richard Gangel
Publication/Sports Illustrated

304 Institutional
Artist/**Harry J. Schaare**
Art Director/Harry J. Schaare
Client/J. Pocker & Son, Inc.

305 Book
Artist/**Richard Brown**
Art Director/Will Winslow
Title/Even the Devil Is Afraid of a Shrew
Publisher/Addison-Wesley Publishing Co.

306 Editorial
Artist/**Isadore Seltzer**
Art Director/Andrew Kner
Publication/Print Magazine

307 Advertising
Artist/Roger Hane
Art Director/George Estes
Client/RCA Records

308 Editorial
Artist/**George Sottung**
Art Director/George Sottung

309 Institutional
Artist/**Cliff Condak**
Art Director/B. Martin Pedersen
Agency/Caldwell Communications
Client/American Airlines

310 Book
Artist/**Fred Pfeiffer**
Art Director/Leonard Leone
Title/The Chinese Art of Healing
Publisher/Bantam Books, Inc.

311 Advertising
Artist/**Bart Forbes**
Art Director/Mike Gaines
Client/Sunoco

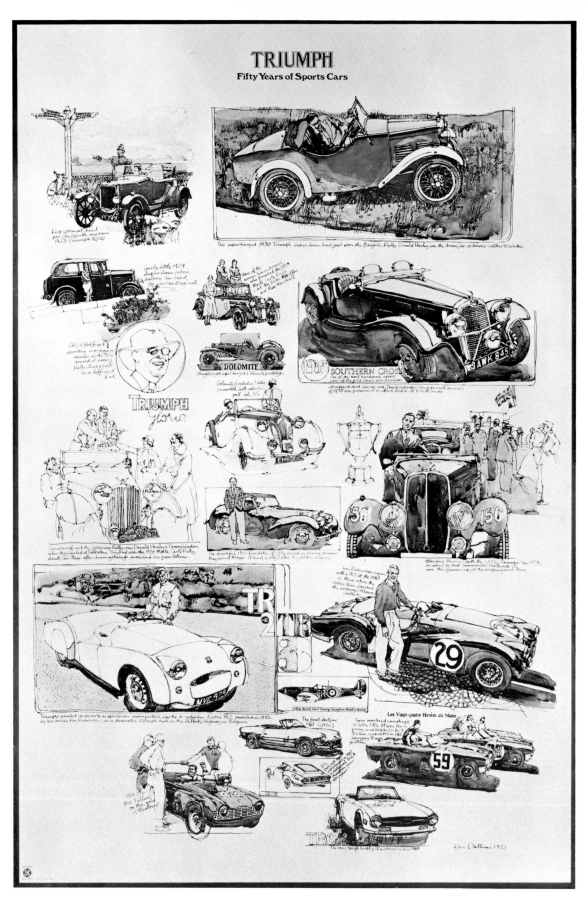

312 Advertising
Artist/**Ken Dallison**
Art Director/Gene Butera
Client/British Leyland
■ **Award of Excellence**

313 Book
Artist/**John Overmyer**
Art Director/Harald Peter
Title/I Am My Brother
Publisher/Hallmark Cards, Inc.

314 Advertising
Artist/**Richard Bober**
Art Director/Art Kaufman & Harry Sehring
Agency/William Douglas McAdams, Inc.
Client/Roche Laboratories

315 Book
Artist/**Etienne Delessert**
Art Director/Etienne Delessert
Title/Kipling Book
Publisher/Doubleday & Co., Inc.

316 Book
Artist/**Ted Rand**
Art Director/Bill Martin, Jr.
Title/Sound of a Young Hunter
Publisher/Holt, Rinehart & Winston, Inc.

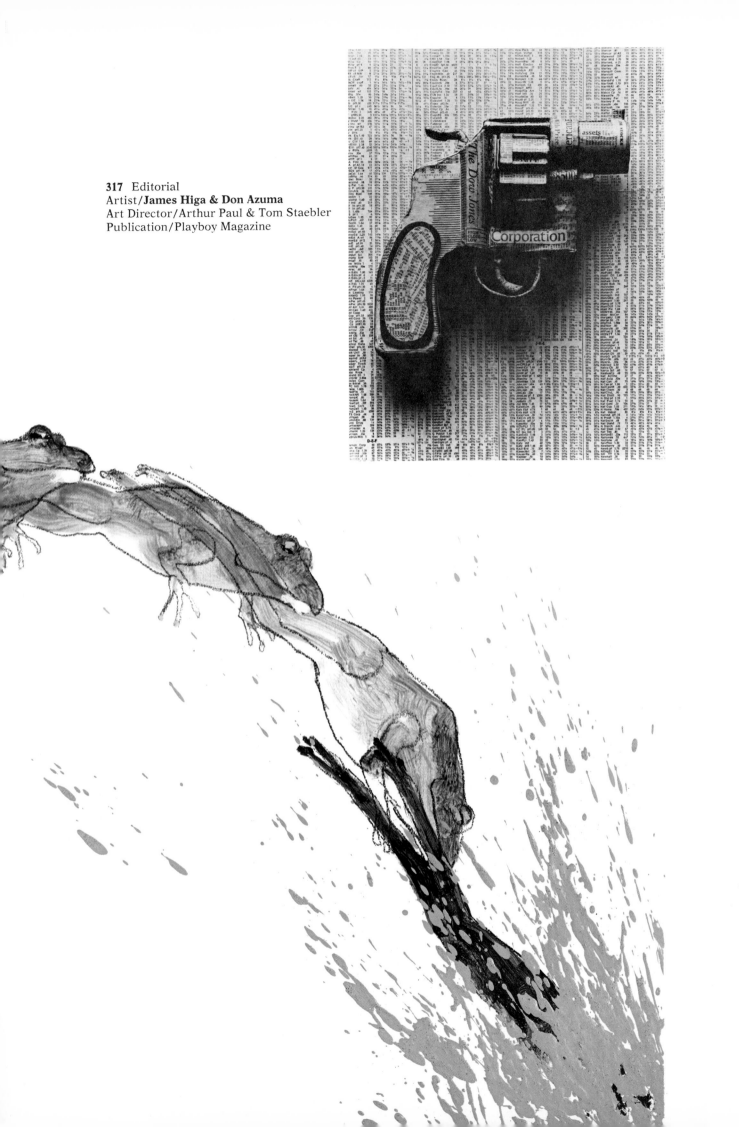

317 Editorial
Artist/**James Higa & Don Azuma**
Art Director/Arthur Paul & Tom Staebler
Publication/Playboy Magazine

318 Institutional
Artist/**Mark Dornan**
Art Director/Mark Dornan

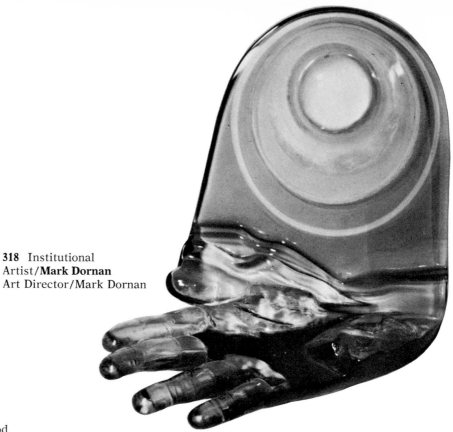

319 Book
Artist/**David Edward Byrd**
Art Director/Harris Lewine
Title/Wit & Wisdom of Hollywood
Publisher/Warner Paperback Library

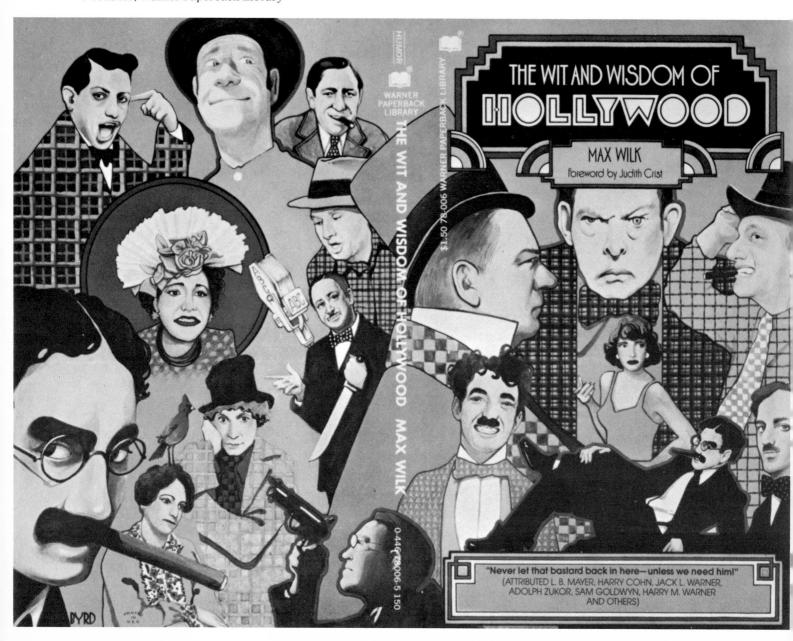

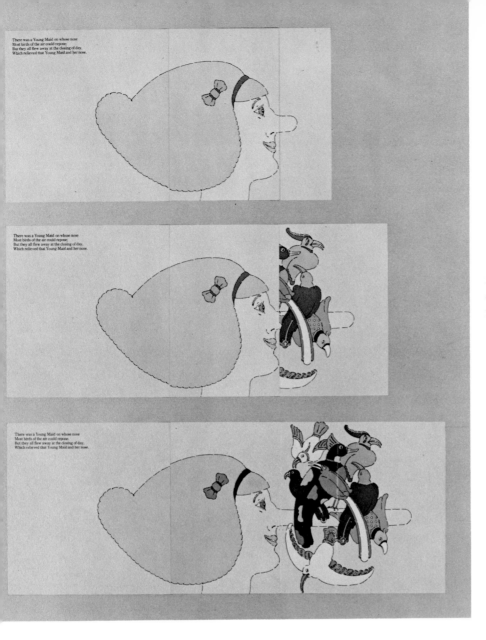

320 Book
Artist/**Seymour Chwast**
Art Director/Mike Frith
Publisher/Random House, Inc.

321 Institutional
Artist/**Paul Melia**
Art Director/Paul Melia

322 Institutional
Artist/**Richard Fish**
Art Director/Richard Fish
Agency/Richard Fish Associates
Client/Volkswagen of America, Inc.

323 Institutional
Artist/**Charles Santore**
Art Director/Bill Oliver
Agency/N.W. Ayer & Son, Inc.
Client/R.O.T.C

324 Editorial
Artist/**Jean Michel Folon**
Art Director/Stan R. Corfman
Publication/Marathon World

325 Editorial
Artist/**Bernie Fuchs**
Art Director/John Newcomb
Publication/Golf Digest, Inc.

326 Book
Artist/**Dickran Palulian**
Art Director/Rallou Malliarakis
Title/New Dimensions II
Publisher/Doubleday & Co., Inc.

327 Book
Artist/**Stan Mack**
Art Director/Mike Frith
Title/"Lonesome Louis" Gordon of Sesame St.
Publisher/Random House, Inc.

When Lonesome Lewis yelled that "Ouch!" people 99 miles away could hear it.

329 Editorial
Artist/**Allan Mardon**
Art Director/Arnold Hoffman
Publication/The New York Times

330 Book
Artist/**Bill Greer**
Art Director/Herb Levitt
Title/Flight Into Danger
Publisher/Random House, Inc.

328 Editorial
Artist/**Lew McCance**
Art Director/Joan Simpson & Lorenzo Garcia
Publisher/Ames Co.

331 Editorial
Artist/**Frank Bozzo**
Art Director/Bob Schaeffer
Publication/Scholastic Magazine

332 Editorial
Artist/**Robert Anthony**
Art Director/Robert Anthony

333 Institutional
Artist/**Brad Holland**
Art Director/Brad Holland

334 Editorial
Artist/**Robert Cunningham**
Art Director/Robert Cunningham

335 Editorial
Artist/**Stan Hunter**
Art Director/Sal Lazzarotti
Publication/Guideposts Magazine

336 Editorial
Artist/**Frank A. Fitzgerald**
Art Director/Ken Deardoff
Publication/Evergreen Review

337 Book
Artist/**Christine Duke**
Art Director/Christine Duke

338 Institutional
Artist/**James Spanfeller**
Art Director/Bill Brockmeir
Client/Phoenix School of Design

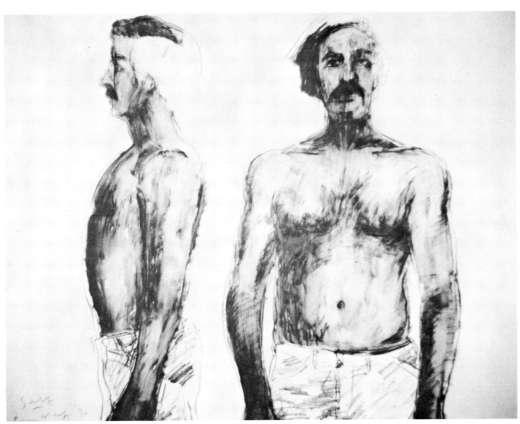

339 Institutional
Artist/**Cliff Condak**
Art Director/Cliff Condak

340 Institutional
Artist/**Bart Forbes**
Art Director/Bart Forbes
Client/Heritage Press

341 Editorial
Artist/**Bernie Fuchs**
Art Director/Robert Hallock
Publication/Lithopinion

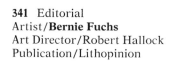

342 Book
Artist/**Roger Hane**
Art Director/Frank Metz
Title/A Separate Reality
Publisher/Simon & Schuster, Inc.

343 Institutional
Artist/**Tom Bailey**
Art Director/Dan Ross

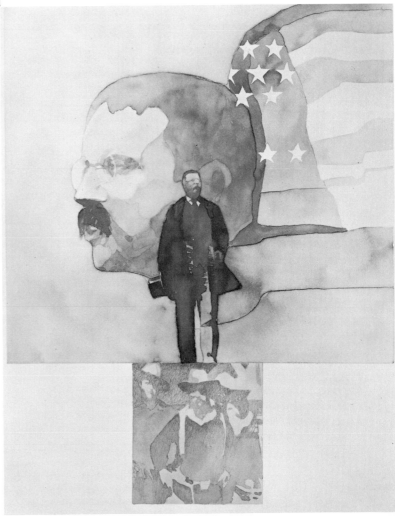

344 Book
Artist/**Etienne Delessert**
Art Director/Etienne Delessert
Title/Kipling Book
Publisher/Doubleday & Co., Inc.

346 Book
Artist/**Ewall Breuer**
Art Director/Barbara Robinson & Linda Bonnett
Title/Field Math Program
Publisher/Field Educational Publications, Inc.

345 Book
Artist/**Ann Lee Polus**
Art Director/Ann Lee Polus
Publisher/David M. Pesanelli, Inc.

347 Advertising
Artist/**Doug Johnson**
Art Director/John Fitzgerald & I. Rothovius
Client/New York Telephone

348 Editorial
Artist/**David Leffel**
Art Director/William F. Cadge
Publication/Redbook Magazine

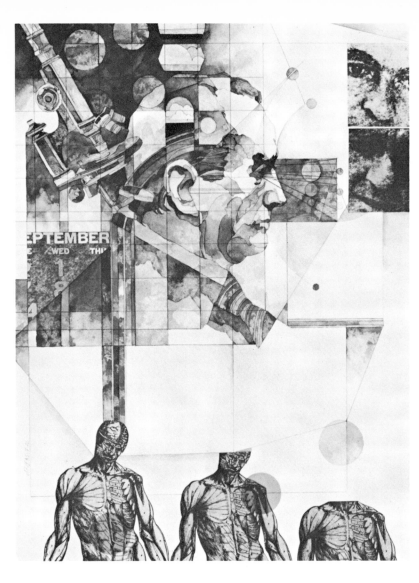

349 Institutional
Artist/**John Freas**
Art Director/Mat Bennett
Agency/Merck, Sharp & Dohme
Client/Merck, Sharp & Dohme

350 Book
Artist/**Bill Morrison**
Art Director/Bill Morrison
Publisher/Scott, Foresman & Co.

351 Advertising
Artist/**Ted CoConis**
Art Director/Donald Smolen
Client/United Artists Corp.

352 Advertising
Artist/**Mark English**
Art Director/Craig Braun
Agency/Wilkes & Braun, Inc.
Client/Ode Records

353 Advertising
Artist/**Gene Szafran**
Art Director/Gene Szafran

354 Institutional
Artist/**Fred Otnes**
Art Director/William Duevell & Henry Epstein
Client/ABC News

355 Book
Artist/**Tom Bailey**
Art Director/Hal Kearney
Title/Accent
Publisher/Scott, Foresman & Co.

356 Editorial
Artist/**Robert Peak**
Art Director/Robert Peak

357 Book
Artist/**Lew McCance**
Art Director/Tom Von Der Linn
Title/Maigrét
Publisher/Reader's Digest Association

358 Book
Artist/**Cliff Condak**
Art Director/Cliff Condak

360 Advertising
Artist/**Carveth Kramer**
Art Director/George Estes
Client/RCA Records

361 Institutional
Artist/**Mark Dornan**
Art Director/Mark Dornan

359 Institutional
Artist/**David M. Gaadt**
Art Director/David M. Gaadt
Agency/Creative Services, Inc.
Client/Creative Services, Inc.

364 Book
Artist/**Roger Kastel**
Art Director/Leonard Leone
Title/Nick Adams Stories
Publisher/Bantam Books, Inc.

365 Book
Artist/**Robert Giusti**
Art Director/Lynn Braswell
Title/Digging It
Publisher/The Dial Press

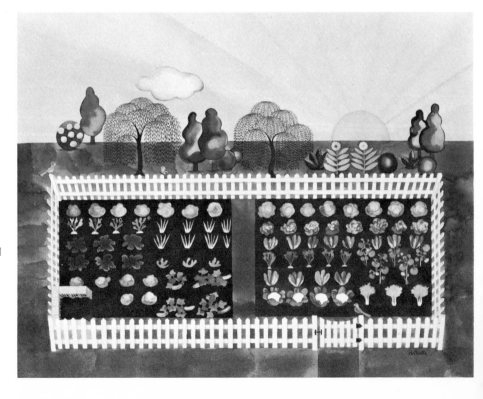

367 Institutional
Artist/**Chet Jezierski**
Art Director/James Dean
Agency/Media Development: NASA
Client/NASA Headquarters

366 Book
Artist/**Susan Swan**
Art Director/Susan Swan

368 Book
Artist/**Robert Byrd**
Art Director/Robert Byrd

369 Editorial
Artist/**Walter Einsel**
Art Director/Harry Redler
Publication/Connecticut Magazine

370 Advertising
Artist/**David McCall Johnston**
Art Director/Arnold Arlow
Agency/Martin Landey Arlow Advertising, Inc.
Client/Coty, Inc.

371 Book
Artist/**Robert Cunningham**
Art Director/Diana Klemin
Title/Drums and Shadows
Publisher/Doubleday & Co., Inc.

372 Advertising
Artist/**Daniel Schwartz**
Art Director/Eugene Kolomatsky
Client/NBC Television

373 Advertising
Artist/**Daniel Schwartz**
Art Director/Eugene Kolomatsky
Client/NBC Television

374 Advertising
Artist/**Edward Sorel**
Art/Director/Andrew Kner
Client/The New York Times

375 Advertising
Artist/**Edward Sorel**
Art Director/Andrew Kner
Client/The New York Times

378 Institutional
Artist/**Bunny Carter**
Art Director/Jim Westbrook
Agency/J. Walter Thompson
Client/Holiday Inn

376 Institutional
Artist/**Jack Unruh**
Art Director/Jimmy Hightower
Client/Johnston Printing

377 Book
Artist/**Lew McCance**
Art Director/Bruce W. Hall
Title/Maggot
Publisher/Paperback Library

ELEGANT FARMER

Welcome to our breakfast table

379 Advertising
Artist/**Bart Forbes**
Art Director/Ziggy Nicholson
Client/Native American League

380 Institutional
Artist/**Robert A. Heindel**
Art Director/Del Martin
Agency/Lord, Sullivan & Yoder
Client/Columbus Coated Fabrics

381 Editorial
Artist/**Barron Storey**
Art Director/Bud Loader
Publication/Flying Magazine

382 Institutional
Artist/**Charles Santore**
Art Director/Bill Oliver
Agency/N.W. Ayer & Sons, Inc.
Client/R.O.T.C.

383 Advertising
Artist/**Stan Hunter**
Art Director/Caroline Waloski
Agency/Kallir, Phillips, Ross, Inc.
Client/McNeil Laboratories, Inc.

384 Editorial
Artist/**Adolph Rosenblatt**
Art Director/Arthur Paul & Kerig Pope
Publication/Playboy Magazine

385 Advertising
Artist/**Robert LoGrippo**
Art Director/George Estes
Client/RCA Records

386 Book
Artist/**Richard Hess**
Art Director/Robert D. Scudellari
Title/A Day No Pigs Would Die
Publisher/Random House, Inc.

387 Advertising
Artist/**David Palladini**
Art Director/Robert E. Hall
Agency/Dean L. Burdick Associates
Client/Winthrop Laboratories

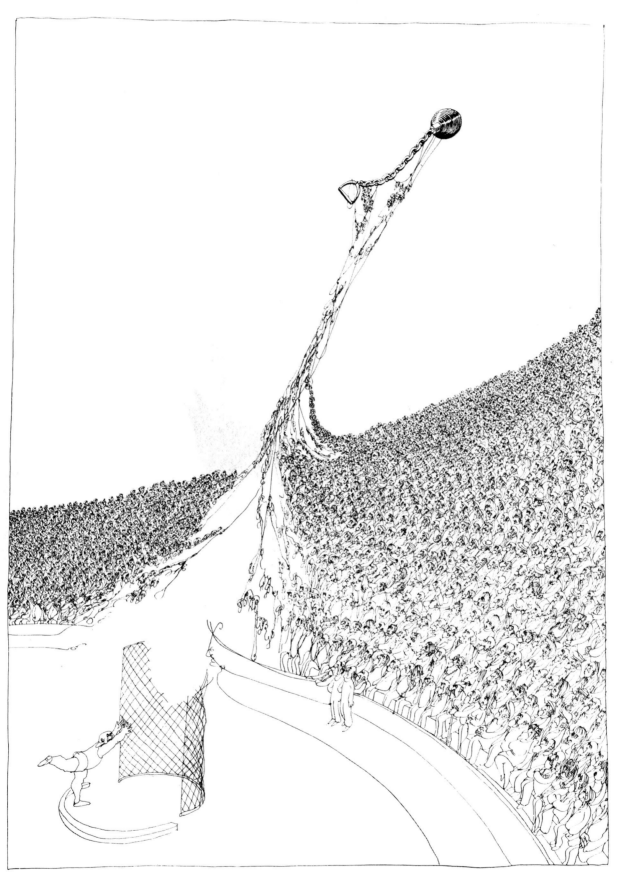

389 Editorial
Artist/**Hans-Georg Rauch**
Art Director/Richard Gangel
Publication/Sports Illustrated

390 Book
Artist/**James Marshall**
Art Director/Walter Lorraine
Title/George and Martha
Publisher/Houghton Mifflin Co.

391 Editorial
Artist/**Robert Shore**
Art Director/Robert Shore

392 Book
Artist/**Gervasio Gallardo**
Art Director/Gervasio Gallardo
■ **Gold Medal**

393 Editorial
Artist/**Lee W. Brubaker**
Art Director/Lee W. Brubaker

394 Advertising
Artist/**George Schwenk**
Art Director/Donald Adamec
Agency/Adamec Associates
Client/J.R. Druid Associates, Inc.

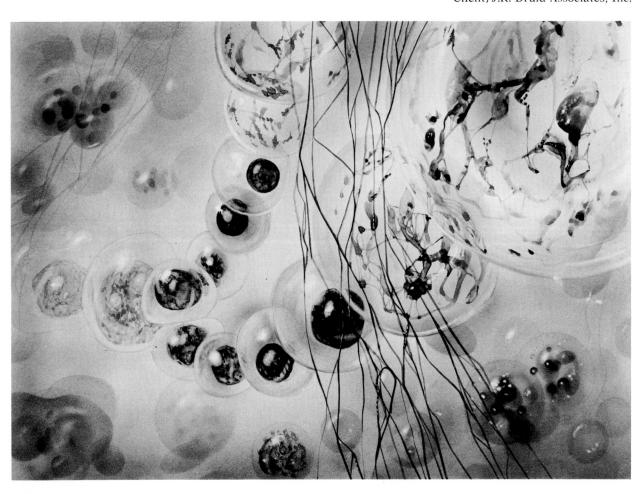

395 Book
Artist/**Bob Jones**
Art Director/Bob Jones

396 Editorial
Artist/**Arson Roje**
Art Director/Arthur Paul & Roy Moody
Publication/Playboy Magazine

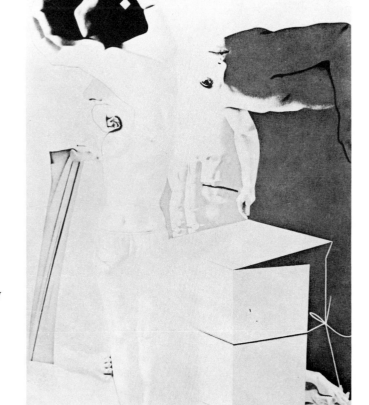

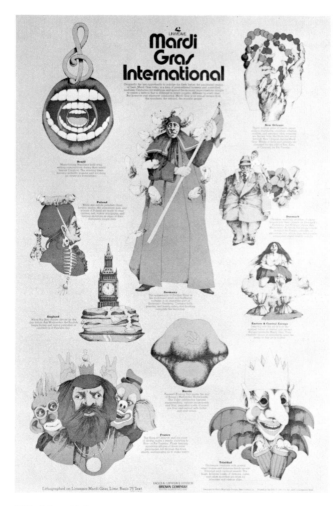

397 Institutional
Artist/**Michael Eagle**
Art Director/Charles McVicker
Client/Society of Illustrators

398 Advertising
Artist/**Ed Lindlof**
Art Director/Charles Steinbaugh
Agency/Harry Mayronne Studios
Client/Brown Paper Co.

399 Institutional
Artist/**Norman Laliberte**
Art Director/John J. Conley
Client/Standard Oil Co. (New Jersey)

400 Advertising
Artist/**Richard Hess**
Art Director/Richard Hess
Agency/Richard Hess & Associates, Inc.
Client/Doubleday & Co., Inc.

401 Advertising
Artist/**Elaine Wozniak**
Art Director/Rossa Cann
Agency/Cargill, Wilson, Acree
Client/PNB of Richmond, Va.

402 Institutional
Artist/**Suzie Fenske**
Art Director/Suzie Fenske

403 Book
Artist/**Dora Leder**
Art Director/Ricky Levinson
Title/No Boys Allowed
Publisher/Science Research Association

404 Institutional
Artist/**Robert Byrd**
Art Director/Robert Byrd

405 Advertising
Artist/**Irwin A. Fleminger**
Art Director/Leonard Restivo
Agency/Bloomingdale's Agency
Client/Bloomingdale's Department Stores

406 Advertising
Artist/**Don Punchatz**
Art Director/Acy Lehman
Client/RCA Records

407 Editorial
Artist/**Paul Giovanopoulos**
Art Director/Len Tossel
Publication/Creative Living

408 Book
Artist/**Christopher Santoro**
Art Director/Christopher Santoro

409 Editorial
Artist/**Robert Cunningham**
Art Director/William F. Cadge
Publication/Redbook Magazine

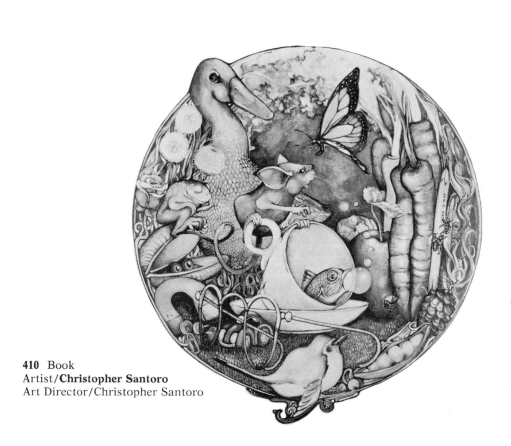

410 Book
Artist/**Christopher Santoro**
Art Director/Christopher Santoro

411 Institutional
Artist/**Tom Bailey**
Art Director/Dan Ross

412 Editorial
Artist/**James Barkley**
Art Director/Modesto Torre
Publication/McCall's Magazine

413 Editorial
Artist/**Thomas B. Allen**
Art Director/Modesto Torre
Publication/McCall's Magazine

414 Editorial
Artist/**Charles McVicker**
Art Director/Curt Schleier
Publication/Travel Scene Magazine

415 Advertising
Artist/**Alan Cober**
Art Director/Herb Barnes
Agency/Klein, Barzman & Hecht
Client/Group W

417 Book
Artist/**Leonard Baskin**
Art Director/Diana Klemin
Title/From the Stone Age to Christianity
Publisher/Doubleday & Co., Inc.

418 Book
Artist/**Gerald McConnell**
Art Director/Bruce W. Hall
Title/A Book of Country Things
Publisher/Paperback Library

16 Book
.rtist/**David Blossom**
.rt Director/Frank Kasa
ublisher/Pyramid Publications

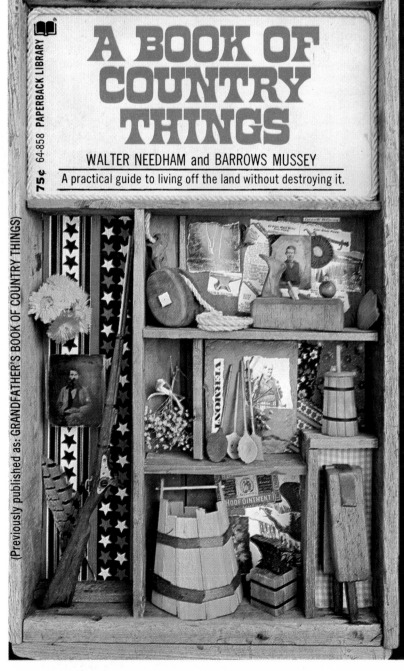

419 Institutional
Artist/**James Barkley**
Art Director/James Barkley
Agency/Our Own Little Studio
Client/U.S. Department of Par

421 Book
Artist/**Howard Rogers**
Art Director/Leonard Leone
Title/The Spiral Road
Publisher/Bantam Books, Inc.

20 Editorial
Artist/**Daniel Schwartz**
Art Director/Seymour Chwast & Milton Glaser
Publication/Audience Magazine

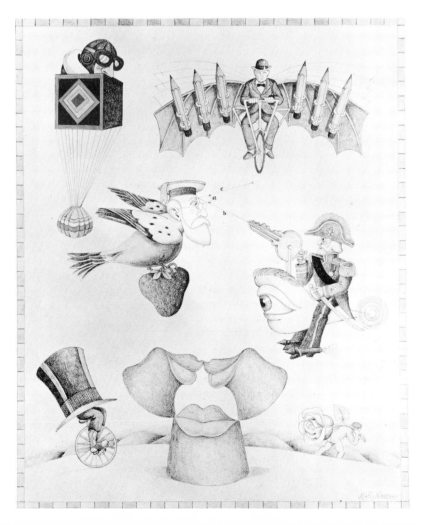

422 Book
Artist/**Marty Norman**
Art Director/Marty Norman

Corporate Financing

VOL. 4, NO. 4   JULY / AUGUST 1972

Pollution
Control
Financing
Grows Up

COLOS

424 Book
Artist/**Frank Frazetta**
Art Director/Charles Volpe
Title/Back To the Stone Age
Publisher/Ace Books
■ **Award of Excellence**

425 Editorial
Artist/**Richard Hess**
Art Director/Richard Hess
Publication/Vista Magazine

426 Advertising
Artist/**Sherry Thompson**
Art Director/Sherry Thompson
Agency/Bracken Smith Advertising
Client/KSL Radio

427 Editorial
Artist/**Daniel Schwartz**
Art Director/Alvin Grossman
Publication/McCall's Magazine
■ **Gold Medal**

428 Editorial
Artist/**Alan Cober**
Art Director/Ira Silberlicht
Publication/Emergency Medicine

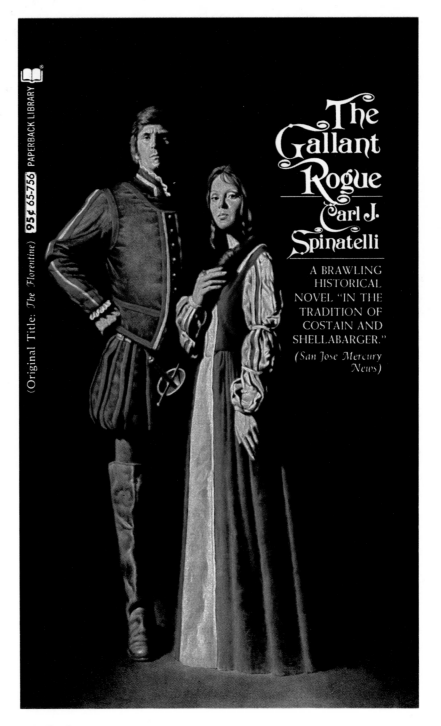

429 Book
Artist/**Peter Caras**
Art Director/Bruce Hall
Title/The Gallant Rogue
Publisher/Paperback Library

430 Institutional
Artist/**Dennis R. Coburn**
Art Director/Dennis R. Coburn

431 Institutional
Artist/**Mort Kunstler**
Art Director/Donald C. Issing
Client/American Cyanamid

432 Book
Artist/**John Berkey**
Art Director/Bob Blanchard
Title/Star #3
Publisher/Ballantine Books, Inc.

WILSON McLEAN

434 Book
Artist/**Wilson McLean**
Art Director/Bob Blanchard
Title/Another Roadside Attraction
Publisher/Ballantine Books, Inc.

433 Advertising
Artist/**Wilson McLean**
Art Director/Craig Braun
Agency/Wilkes & Braun, Inc.
Client/Ode Records

435 Advertising
Artist/**Roger Hane**
Art Director/Art Kaufman & Harry Sehring
Agency/William Douglas McAdams, Inc.
Client/Roche Laboratories

436 Institutional
Artist/**Don Ivan Punchatz**
Art Director/Barbara Bertoli
Client/Darwin Bahm

437 Book
Artist/**Daniel Maffia**
Art Director/Ken Sneider & Nick Calabrese
Title/King Lear
Publisher/Reader's Digest Association

438 Editorial
Artist/**Charles Santore**
Art Director/Jerry Alten
Publication/TV Guide Magazine

439 Editorial
Artist/**Joe Bowler**
Art Director/Herbert Bleiweiss
Publication/Ladies' Home Journal

440 Editorial
Artist/**John Mardon**
Art Director/Max Newton
Publication/Weekend Magazine

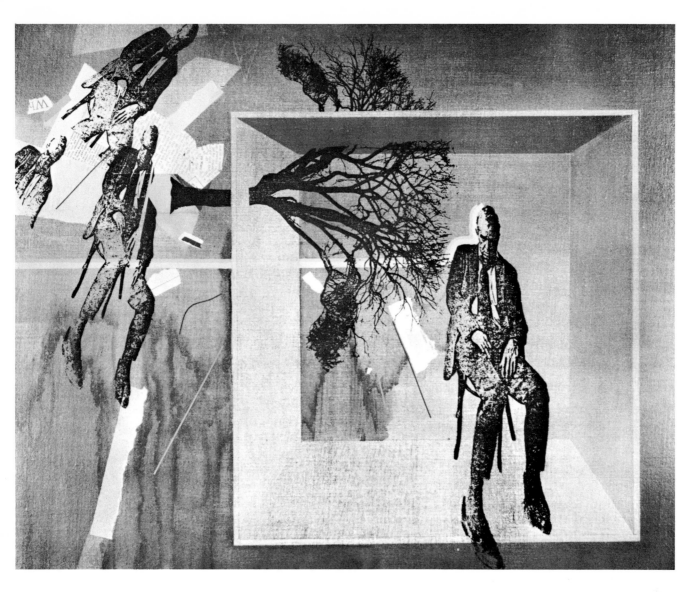

441 Editorial
Artist/**Fred Otnes**
Art Director/Bob Clive
Publication/Life Magazine

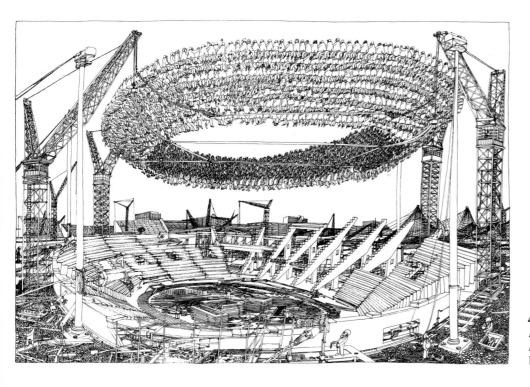

442 Editorial
Artist/**Hans-Georg Rauch**
Art Director/Richard Gangel
Publication/Sports Illustrated

くにを萩屋

443 Editorial
Artist/**Kunio Hagio**
Art Director/Arthur Paul & Kerig Pope
Publication/Playboy Magazine

444 Editorial
Artist/**Bart Forbes**
Art Director/Joan Fenton
Publication/Seventeen Magazine

445 Editorial
Artist/**Anita Siegel**
Art Director/William F. Cadge
Publication/Redbook Magazine

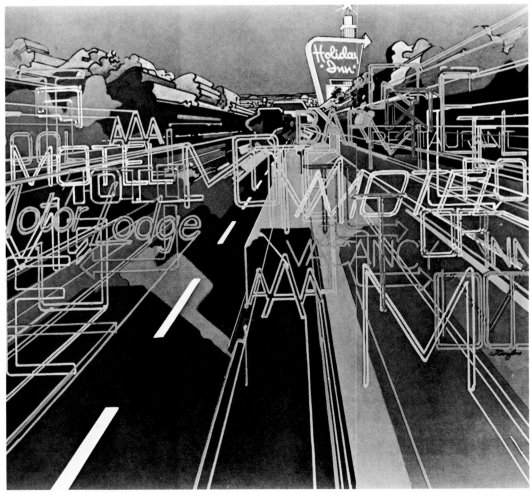

446 Editorial
Artist/**Arno Sternglass**
Art Director/Milton Glaser
Publication/Audience Magazine

447 Book
Artist/**Gilbert Stone**
Art Director/Robert Reed
Title/House of All Nations
Publisher/Holt, Rinehart and Winston, In

448 Book
Artist/**George Guzzi**
Art Director/George Guzzi

449 Institutional
Artist/**Fred Otnes**
Art Director/William Duevell & Henry Epstein
Client/ABC News

450 Institutional
Artist/**Joseph Scrofani**
Art Director/Joseph Scrofani

451 Advertising
Artist/**Dennis Luczak**
Art Director/Dennis Luczak

452 Editorial
Artist/**Hans-Georg Rauch**
Art Director/Richard Gangel
Publication/Sports Illustrated

453 Book
Artist/**Robert Heindel**
Art Director/James Plumeri
Title/The Loneliness of the Long Distance Runner
Publisher/New American Library

454 Book
Artist/**Don Ivan Punchatz**
Art Director/Bill Rose
Title/Prehistoric Animals
Publisher/Time-Life Books

455 Book
Artist/**Robert LoGrippo**
Art Director/Annika Umans
Title/Forgotten Dreams
Publisher/Houghton Mifflin Co.

456 Institutional
Artist/**Chet Jezierski**
Art Director/James Dean
Agency/Media Development: NASA
Client/NASA Headquarters

457 Advertising
Artist/**Roger Hane**
Art Director/Alan J. Klawans
Client/Smith, Kline & French Laboratories

458 Editorial
Artist/**David Savage**
Art Director/David Dolson
Publication/Detroit Free Press

459 Editorial
Artist/**Fred Otnes**
Art Director/Robert Hallock
Publication/Lithopinion

460 Advertising
Artist/**Phil Hayes**
Art Director/Len Obsatz
Agency/Sudler & Hennessey, Inc.

461 Editorial
Artist/**Liam Roberts**
Art Director/Liam Roberts

462 Book
Artist/**David Edward Byrd**
Art Director/Howard Winters
Title/The Devine Sarah
Publisher/Lancer Books, Inc.

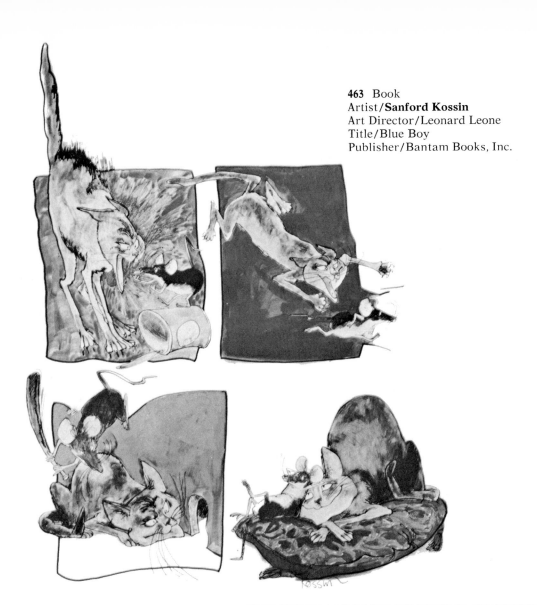

463 Book
Artist/**Sanford Kossin**
Art Director/Leonard Leone
Title/Blue Boy
Publisher/Bantam Books, Inc.

464 Institutional
Artist/**Robert A. Heindel**
Art Director/Del Martin
Agency/Lord, Sullivan & Yoder
Client/Columbus Coated Fabrics

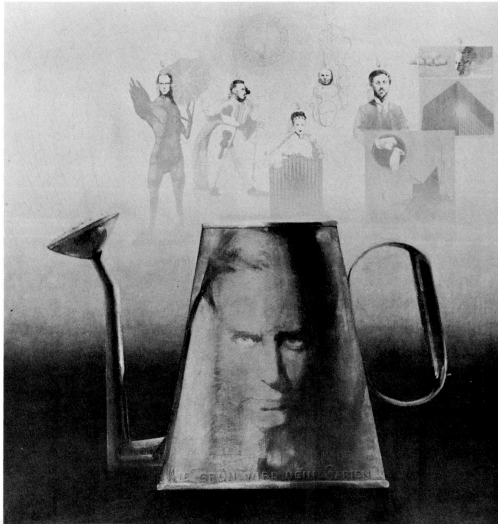

465 Book
Artist/**Jim Conahan**
Art Director/Jim Conahan

466 Editorial
Artist/**Christine Duke**
Art Director/Christine Duke

Index

While every effort has been made to insure the accuracy of the credits in this volume, it is inevitable that an occasional error may have crept in. On behalf of the Society of Illustrators, the publishers would appreciate information about any omissions or corrections. As this book is printed in process colors, we regret that the original colors of some of the illustrations reproduced here have been altered.

Production Credits

The text in this book is:
Aster with Bold

Composition by:
M.J. Baumwell, Typography

Offset plates and printing by:
Connecticut Printers, Inc.

Advertisements section by:
Bodley Printers, Inc.

The paper is:
Mead's Black and White Offset Enamel Dull

Paper supplier:
Andrews/Nelson/Whitehead Publishing Papers

Binding cloth by:
G.S.B. Fabrics Corp.

Bound by:
A. Horowitz & Son

Jacket printed by:
Princeton Polychrome Press

Production Supervision:
Lee Tobin, Hastings House

Assistant to the publisher:
James Moore, Hastings House

Illustrators 15

ILLUSTRATORS

ART DIRECTORS

CLIENTS

TITLES

Advertisements

Jane Sneyd, *Advertising Director.*

Illustrators 15

JIM CROWELL • ANGELA FERNAN • MAMORU FUNAI • DENVER GILLEN • JUDY GLASSER • RISA GLICKMAN • DENMAN HAMPSON • ... MURDOCCA • MIKE NAKAI • KELLY OECHSLI • BOB OWENS • CARL OWENS • JUDY PELIKAN • TED RAND • GILBERT RISWOLD • TONIA HAMPSON • TOM HILL • NICOLE HOLLANDER • JUDY KANIS • CAROLE KOWALCHUK • DICK KRAMER • MARION KRUPP • VALDIS KUPRIS • ROBERTA LANGMAN • PETER LEHNDORFF • YEE LIN • KEN LONGTEMPS • ANITA LOVITT • ELEANOR MILL • VICTOR MOJICA • CARL MOLNO • DALE MOYER • SAL MURDOCCA • MARGARET CRANSTOUN • BOB CRAM • OLIVIA H. H. COLE • MARILYN COHEN • RICHARD BROWN • BRIAN BOURKE • DOROTHEA SIERRA • JOEL SNYDER • ZINA SURCHUK • JOHN SWATSLEY • SUSANNE VALLA • VICTOR VALLA • CHARLES WALKER • RON WALOTSKY • MICHAEL WOOD • PHOTOGRAPHY • CURTIS BLAKE • JOEL GORDON • MICHEL HERON • JOAN MENSCHENFREUND • GEORGE ROOS • JOEL WELTMAN • ROBERT ALTEMUS • ROBERT SHORE • CHARLES SHAW • IRIS SCHWEITZER • DEN SCHOFIELD • JOEL SCHICK • ROZ SCHANZER • HARRY SCHAARE • CHRISTOPHER SANTORO • FREYA SAGLIMBENI • ILLUSTRATION • A COMPLETE SERVICE TO PUBLISHERS IN DESIGN, ILLUSTRATION AND PRODUCTION

SAL MURDOCCA

© craven & evans CREATIVE GRAPHICS

443 PARK AVE. SOUTH, NEW YORK, N.Y. 10016, TELEPHONE (212) 889-8616

artists

NORMAN ADAMS / KEVIN BROOKS / DAVID BYRD / BOB HANDVILLE
NORMAN LALIBERTE / JIM MANOS / JACK MARTIN / FRED OTNES / GENE SZAFRAN
REPRESENTED BY BILL ERLACHER / LESLEY LOGUE
ARTISTS ASSOCIATES / 211 E. 51 ST. / NEW YORK, N.Y. 10022 / 212 755-1365/6

Wilson McLean
also appears in
Sports Illustrated

THE TALENTS OF FRANCO ACCONERO / GEORGE ALVARO / JOHN ASARO
JIM AVATI / PAUL BACON / BOB BAXTER / HARRY BENNETT
IRVING BERNSTEIN / BOB BERRAN / EDGAR BLAKENEY / DAVE BLOSSOM
IRVING BOGEN / STAN BORACK / JACK BRESLOW / DAN BROWN
JAMES CALVIN / PETER CARAS / JOHN CHILLY / TED COCONIS / GIL COHEN
JEFF CORNELL / BOB CUEVAS / ANN DALTON / WHITNEY DARROW Jr.
JACK DAVIS / LEO AND DIANE DILLON / ELAINE DUILLO / DEAN ELLIS
TONY FERRARA / RITA FLODEN / FRANK FRAZETTA / STAN GALLI
HECTOR GARRIDO / CHARLIE GEHM / GEORGE GIUSTI / TONY GRECO
NORMAN GREEN / JOAN GREENFIELD / GEORGE GROSS / BLAKE HAMPTON
CARL HANTMAN / JOHNNY HART / BOB HEINDEL / BILL HOFFMAN
MIKE HOOKS / CHET JEZIERSKI / BILL JOHNSON / JEFF JONES / ALLAN KASS
STUART KAUFMAN / BIL KEANE / HANK KETCHAM / STAN KLIMLEY
HILARY KNIGHT / DICK KOHFIELD / SANDY KOSSIN / LESTER KRAUSS
LARRY KRESEK / MORT KUNSTLER / PAUL LEHR / BIRNEY LETTICK
MUNI LIEBLEIN / OSCAR LIEBMAN / JOE LOMBARDERO / MIKE LUDLOW
JOHN McDERMOTT / BOB McGINNIS / ED McLAUGHLIN / ALAN MAGEE
MICHELE MALDEAU / SAUL MANDEL / LOU MARCHETTI / ALAN MARDON
JOHN MELO / TOM MILLER / CHARLIE MOLL / DON MOSS
ZENOWIJI ONYSHKEWYCH / JERRY PODWIL / WALTER POPP / DICK POWERS
VICTOR PREZIO / DON PUNCHATZ / DORIS RODEWIG / HOWARD ROGERS
ARNOLD ROTH / HARRY SCHAARE / ELLIOT SCHNEIDER / CORNELIUS SCHOLL
BOB SCHULZ / SUSAN SCHWALB / SHANNON STERNWEIS / JIM SHARPE
HAL SEIGEL / GEORGE SOTTUNG / DON STIVERS / WALTER STORCK
MIKE STROMBERG / DARREL SWEET / GENE SZAFRAN / HERB TAUSS
BILL TEASON / BARNEY THOMPSON / JACK THURSTON / BILL WENZEL
ANN WOLF **APPEAR ON FAWCETT PAPERBACK COVERS.**

|FAWCETT|

CREST / PREMIER / GOLD MEDAL / 1515 BROADWAY / NEW YORK CITY / 10036

REPRESENTING OVER 50 ILLUSTRATORS

**COMPLETE GRAPHIC DESIGN AND PRODUCTION
OF JUVENILE AND EDUCATIONAL MATERIALS (a staff of 20)
WRITE FOR FREE ART BUYERS GUIDE**

PUBLISHERS
GRAPHICS
611 RIVERSIDE AVE.
WESTPORT, CONN.
06880 • 203-226-3505

SHOWCASE

For 20 years you've helped make PLAYBOY an illustrator's showcase.
We hope you'll continue.

Submit your samples to:
Editorial Art Department
Playboy Magazine, 10th Floor
919 North Michigan Avenue
Chicago, Illinois 60611

(Mail slides or photographs only — no original art, please.)

Behind the truly outstanding art you'll

ind Frank and Jeff Lavaty.

BFA degree programs in Fine Arts, Communication Design, Fashion Design, Environmental Design, Illustration and Art Education. Parsons School of Design* is an accredited member of the Middle States Association of Colleges and Secondary Schools and the National Association of Schools of Art. Parsons operates under absolute charter from the Board of Regents of the State of New York.

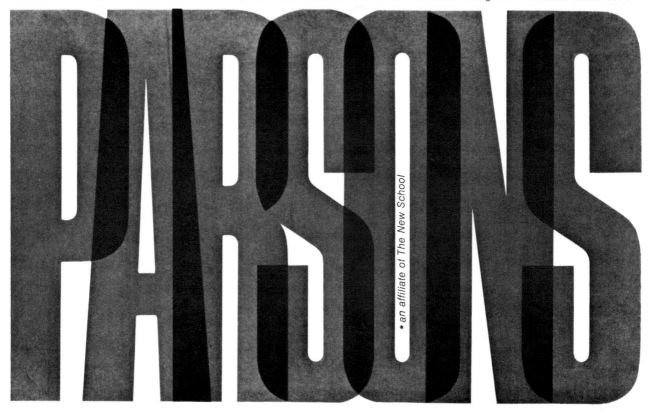

*an affiliate of The New School

THE PENROSE GRAPHIC ARTS INTERNATIONAL ANNUAL

SINCE 1895. acknowledged as the leading international commentator and recorder of changes in taste and fashion in the graphic arts.

The 1974 edition, Volume 67 in this series, will again reflect a broad range of interests for designers as well as technical developments. Sumptuously produced as always with many examples in full color.

Published each year in May, now in association with Northwood Publications, Ltd., London by

VISUAL COMMUNICATION BOOKS • HASTINGS HOUSE, PUBLISHERS
New York 10016

We hope we're in your book

Artists International

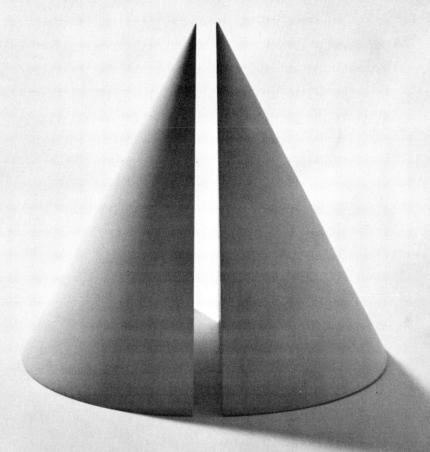

Representing exceptional illustrators in the field of
advertising, editorial and institutional communications.

John Alcorn	Robert Fillie
Patrick Blackwell	Roberto Innoncenti
Frank Brugos	Laszlo Kubinyi
Philip Castle	Norman MacDonald
Sal Catalano	Jennifer Perrott
Tony Chen	Michael Turner
Heather Cooper	Allen Welkis

Artists International 67 E. 80th Street, New York, New York, 10021 Michael G. Brodie (212) 249-5760

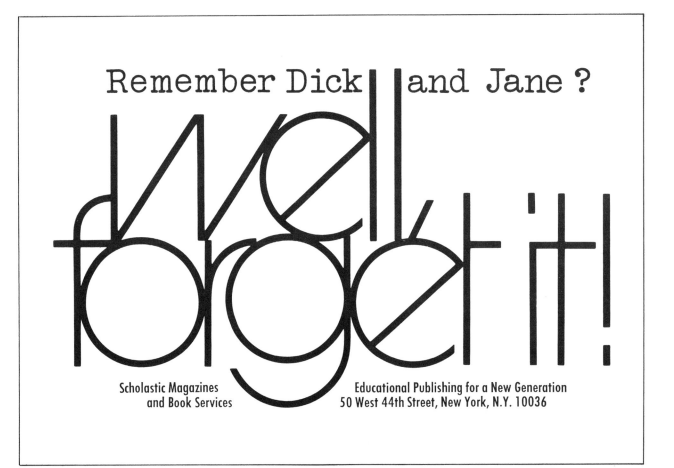

Pelikan PASTEL-COLORED CHALKS
12-stick, assorted-colors set. Also sets of one color.

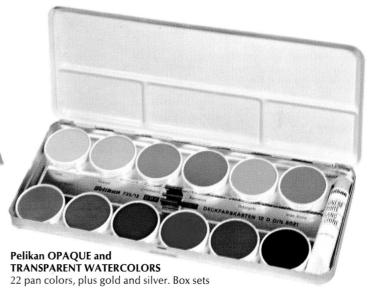

Pelikan DESIGNERS COLORS
69 brilliant colors in 1 oz. and 1/3-oz. tubes, 1 oz. jars, plus 4 metallics in jars. Dry to rich, opaque finish on paper, wood, textile, many surfaces. 12-color set of 1/3-oz. tubes. Ask for color chart.

Pelikan PLAKA CASEIN COLORS
Excellent coverage on glass, metal, paper, other surfaces. Matte-velvet waterproof finish. 25 beautiful shades, also gold and silver metallics, 7 fluorescents. 2-oz. jars or 12-oz. tins. 17 shades in 9 1/2-oz. spray cans. 6-color hobby set. Ask for color chart.

Pelikan GRAPHIC WHITE
Excellent coverage. Flat matte finish. Dilutable. 1-oz. tubes and 2-oz. jars. Also black in tubes.

Pelikan OPAQUE and TRANSPARENT WATERCOLORS
22 pan colors, plus gold and silver. Box sets of 6, 12 and 24 replaceable pan colors, plus tube of white. Ask for literature.

Pelikan ARTIST BRUSHES High quality selection at reasonable cost. Ask for literature.

Pelikan

... for 130 years, creators of color concentrations so rich, so lavish they are an inspiration for work of enduring beauty. That's why Pelikan artist colors are used worldwide.

Pelikan offers a full range of ink formulations for predictable, dependable results: Waterproof drawing inks in rich black and 15 vibrant transparent colors, 1 oz. or 2/5th oz. bottle; 6 permanent opaque colors, 1 oz. or 1/2 pt. bottle; also non-waterproof Pelikan Fount India, 1 1/4 oz. or 1/2 pt. bottle. Write for color charts.

KOH-I-NOOR

AVAILABLE THROUGH YOUR PREFERRED DEALER
Koh-I-Noor Rapidograph, Inc., 100 North Street, Bloomsbury, N.J. 08804
In Canada: Koh-I-Noor/Canada/Ltd., 4180 Ave. de Courtrai, Montreal 249, Quebec

Artists' Representatives
331 East 50th Street
New York, New York 10022
212-Plaza 3-5146

helen wohlberg inc.

Angela Adams
William H. Amos
Robert Binks
Herbert Danska
Beatrice Darwin
Rosalie Davidson
Joan Drescher
Alex Ebel
Lois Ehlert
Rosalind Fry
Tom Funk
Nahid Haghighat
Hilary Hayton
Rosekrans Hoffman
Gerry Hoover
Fred Irvin
Harvey Kidder
Gordon Laite
Donald Leake
Dora Leder
Ronald LeHew
Don Madden
Stefan Martin
Erica Merkling
Jane Nelson
Nickzad Nodjoumi
Lilian Obligado
Susan Perl
Jan Pyk

Barry Rubin
Douglas Snow
Arvis L. Stewart
Phero Thomas
John Wallner
Christine Westerberg
Meg Wohlberg

helen wohlberg
frances means

OUR DOOR IS ALWAYS OPEN

Artwork is an essential part of our business, and during the course of years we have worked with some of the most distinguished artists, illustrators and designers in the world. At the right is a partial list.

Western Publishing Company, Inc., through its various divisions, publishes and prints a wide variety of books for adults and children, as well as periodicals, educational material, games, playing cards, toys and other packaged items.

Our door is always open to creative people. Write, call, or drop in at any of our offices in New York, Los Angeles, or Racine, Wisconsin.

Western Publishing Company, Inc.

Publishing imprints: GOLDEN PRESS • WHITMAN

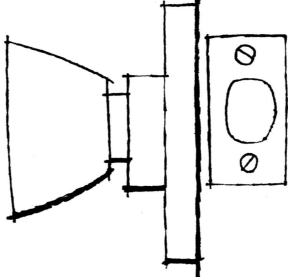

John Alcorn
Joan Anglund
Aurelius Battaglia
Shielah Beckett
Ludwig Bemmelmans
Harry Bennett
Eugene Berman
Lawrence Bjorklund
Mary Blair
Bob Blechman
Eric Blegvad
Niels Bodecker
Seymour Chwast
Herbert Danska
Cornelius DeWitt
Ann Ophelia Dowden
Gertrude Elliot
Dean Ellis
Robert Fawcett
Helen Federico
Betty Fraser
Antonio Frasconi
Gyo Fujikawa
Tibor Gergerly
George Giusti
Denver Gillen
Lou Glanzman
Milton Glaser
Simon Greco
Charles Harper
Don Helm
Homer Hill
Clark Hulings
Scott Johnston
Carroll Jones
Leonard Kalish
Joe Kaufman
Howard Koslow
Robert Kuhn
Robert J. Lee
James Lewicki
Walter Linsenmaier
Harry McNaught
Tran Mawicke
Rebecca Merrilees
John Paar Miller
Yoko Mitsuhashi
Susan Perl
Barry Phillips
Richard Powers
Alice and Martin Provensen
Albert John Pucci
Harlow Rockwell
Feodor Rojankovsky
Richard Scarry
Dan Schwartz
Ben Shahn
Robert Shore
Arthur Singer
Lawrence Beale Smith
Edward Sorrell
Peter Spier
David Stone
William Teason
Gustav Tenggrenn
Murray Tinkelman
Alton Tobey
Leonard Weisgard
Eloise Wilkin
Garth Williams
Rudy Zallinger

the **Quinlan** artwork co. ltd.

A Fox is quick (0 to 50 in 10 seconds). It's surefooted (front-wheel drive). This sly, cunning sedan can take the sharpest turns nimbly (sports car type steering and suspension). It can stop straight in its tracks (special braking/steering systems). And it doesn't eat much (23 miles per gallon). Best of all, for under $3,400* you can catch the Fox.

YOUR HUNT IS OVER. THE QUICK, SLY, CRAFTY,

CUNNING FOX BY AUDI IS HERE.

P12-4590

45c 51st New York

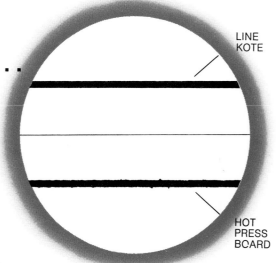

✕ CAMBRIC ✕

Options Beckett Cambric is stocked in custom-cut sizes as well as standard large-press sizes. And its price won't shoot holes in your budget.

Protect your weapons
Enclose your printed piece in a matching Cambric envelope. No. 10 and Monarch sizes are available for prompt delivery.

fig 2

Finish it off Cambric's linen-like finish has a neat, crisp appearance. Ask your Beckett merchant for a sample book today. Don't wait until you're under the gun.

Beckett
THE BECKETT PAPER COMPANY • HAMILTON, OHIO

This is BECKETT CAMBRIC, Gray, 70 lb.

ANNOUNCING—The First Annual of European Editorial, Book, Advertising, Television, Cinema and Design Art

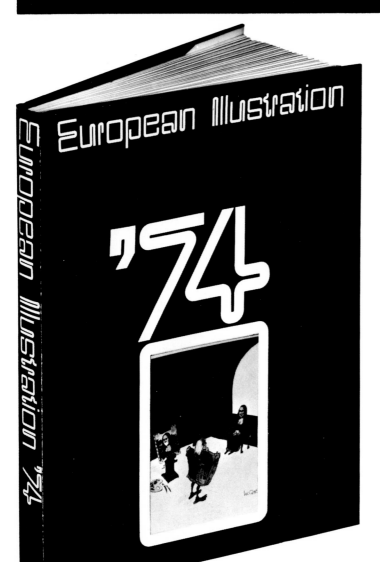

Drawing its material from the widest range of European mass media, this is an unparalleled showcase for the versatile talents of the leading artists and illustrators at work in Europe today. Edited by Edward Booth-Clibborn, founder member and chairman of the Designers and Art Directors Association, London.

About 224 pages, 9" x 11", with 350 subjects, 40 to 50 in color. Price to be announced.

European Illustration '74

will be published June/July in association with the British publisher, Constable & Co., Ltd. by

VISUAL COMMUNICATION BOOKS

Hastings House, Publishers • New York 10016

Join the Club